The Complete Book of
ARCHERY

Proof that bowfishing can be more than child's play. Here Bob Lee of Wing Archery Co. exhibits an alligator bagged with a 65-pound Red Wing Hunter bow.

The Complete Book

of ARCHERY

by Robert Gannon

Coward-McCann, Inc. New York

Contents

6 CONTENTS

Appendix

$Preface$

DESPITE the fact that the bow and arrow was the principal weapon of war for 300 years
—and in sixteenth-century England is was mandatory that every physically able male own and use a bow
—and before gunpowder was invented the bow was the main hunting implement in nearly every society in the world
. . . there are now more archers in the world than at any time before in history.

Today some 7½ million Americans participate in archery to the extent of at least $32 million each year. According to *Sporting Goods Dealer*, spokesman for the industry, archery equipment ranked fourth in dollar volume in 1963—ahead of camping equipment, tennis supplies, firearms, and golf equipment. Nearly 10,000 field tournaments are now being registered annually with the National Field Archery Association. The Archery Institute estimates that in 1962 some 3½ million archers participated in tournaments, and over 320,000 archers went bowhunting.

All of which goes to show that archery is a big thing in the U. S. today. And it's getting bigger all the time. Indoor archery "lanes," for example—the hottest thing to happen to the sport since fiberglass—are opening at the rate of two a week; one company's goal is to open 5,000 in the next five years. These electronically operated shooting complexes, according to spokesmen in the sports industry, may very well catapult archery into as big an indoor participating sport as bowling.

In this book I have tried to answer all the questions asked by both new and experienced archers. In doing so, I found that I was beginning to ask questions myself. And the answers were not always easy to find. So I went to champions, bowhunters, manufacturers, equipment repair specialists, organization committeemen, and plain everyday hobbyists. Many of these helpers are acknowledged in the text. Most aren't. Roy Bucklew, for example, who was kind enough to extend me hospitality at his home in the Florida Keys while I pulled the book together. And my wife, June, who put up with my bow and me all these years.

I'd like to take time out right now to thank the experts who so kindly checked my chapters for accuracy:

Chapter 1—Walter Chersack, President, the New Jersey Archery Association.

Chapter 2—Carl Moore, history graduate student at Rutgers, The State University, New Brunswick, N. J.

Chapter 3—Frank H. Scott, for Colt's Patent Fire Arms Mfg. Co.

Chapter 4—Cliff Zwickey, President, Zwickey Archery Co.

Chapter 5—Robert C. Bennett, President, L. C. Whiffen Co., Inc.

Chapter 6—C. A. Saunders, President, Saunders Archery Target Co.

Chapter 7—Various executives of the Shakespeare Company.

Chapter 8—Wayne L. Aitken, Southern Regional Manager, Colt's Patent Fire Arms Mfg. Co.

Chapter 9—Larkin (Buck) Powell, President, S-K-A Scope Mount, Inc.

Chapter 10—Earl Hoyt, Jr., President, Hoyt Archery Company.

Chapter 11—Members of Lincoln Park Archers, Towaco, N. J.

Chapter 12—Various executives of Ben Pearson, Inc.

Chapter 13—George E. Rohrbach, Acting Secretary, National Field Archery Association.

✿ ✿ ✿ ✿ ✿

If you are a beginning archer, I recommend that you read each how-to-shoot section completely before attempting to do whatever it's talking about. And *then* go out to the field and follow the instructions point by point.

For purposes of clarity—to say nothing of writing ease—I have assumed in most cases that everyone who reads this is right-handed and male. If you are neither, don't despair. Left-handers, using left-handed bows, who simply substitute "left" for "right" in the text should have no trouble. And neither should women who have bows of the right strength —except in such obvious situations—close draw, for instance —where physique plays a part (if the Amazons' solution doesn't appeal).

On reflection, I have the feeling that I've stressed the division of archery into two camps—field and target—more than I should have. I suggest that while you read, you remember that archery is a *single* sport, that many archers are both target and field men, and that with few exceptions, techniques, equipment, even attitude of the two are identical.

Bowhunters will note that no single chapter is devoted to hunting; instead, hunting references are sprinkled throughout. There are several reasons for this. In the first place, good books on bowhunting are now on the market; most of what I have to say would merely have been embellishment. In the second, there isn't as much difference as you might think between hunting with a bow and a gun—except that with a bow you have to be just that much better. And finally, though a large number of bowhunters roam the woods each year, most archers who think about hunting do only that— think about it; they never actually get out in the woods and shoot at animals.

Incidentally, there once was a fair amount of antagonism between gun hunters and bowhunters. This is no longer the case except in isolated instances. The National Rifle Association, in fact, publishes archery literature, and many hunters shoot with guns one month, bows the next.

One point I'd like to underline, something emphasized throughout the book: relax. Take it easy. If you're not the greatest, who cares? Be as free from tension and strain as you can when you shoot. Archery is—or should be—fun. And with you relaxed, your score might, just might, skyrocket.

To the experienced bowman I offer my apologies for what will seem much tediousness when it comes to essentials. But you probably have forgotten what those first dozen trips to the range were like. When you come to something in the text you already know, run over it quickly, but don't skip it entirely. Hopefully, you will find items of surprise. Just one little idea that you've never heard before might make all the difference in your future scores.

Finally, I would like to say that this book was not designed to be left on the end table for company to look through, nor to be stuck up in the glass-fronted bookcase and removed only occasionally to settle an argument. Rather, it is designed as a tool. But a tool in itself is worthless; it becomes useful only when put to work. So toss this volume into your tackle box, underline things you want to remember, make nasty comments in the margin where you disagree. If, years from now, I see copies mud-spattered, marked up and dog-eared, I'll be gratified, for chances are *those* books will have achieved their objective.

ROBERT GANNON

Islamorada, Florida Keys
Summer, 1963

Chapter 1

WHY BOTHER?

ARCHERY is an awful lot of trouble, really. In order to come anywhere near your target you must be in fairly good physical shape, know your equipment, have spent hours practicing, and you must even have a working knowledge—if subconscious—of physics. And for what? To send a projectile across a distance to strike a target—something that, for the most part, can be done much better with a gun.

But not always. The Pacific Telephone Company, for instance, uses bows to shoot telephone lines across poison oak- and rattlesnake-infested canyons 400 feet wide. Naturalists in a northern forest shoot bears with hypodermic-syringe-tipped arrows, then attach tiny transmitters to the animals in an effort to find out where they spend the winter. In Chicago, a catman prowler used a bow to send a rope ladder into second-story windows.

Those things can't very well be done by firearms. It's doubtful, though, that you ever will put your bow-shooting technique to such uses. What, then, will you get out of all the trouble?

In the first place, archery is a hobby that will get you out in the fresh air; if you need an excuse to take to the fields, this is it. And while you're out in all that openness, you're exercising. You use chest, back, shoulder and upper arm muscles a less fortunate person doesn't even know he owns.

You learn to use them correctly, too, and your newly ac-
quired coordination may even wash over into your non-
archery movements. Shoot a double American target round
and you'll walk nearly two miles. What's more, because
you're stretching your chest, you're breathing for a change.
And your hands are so busy you cut down on your smoking.
Further, bending over to look for arrows puts you in positions you'd never assume behind a desk or in front of the TV
set.

If the shooting is done correctly, a half hour of backyard
archery is equal to the exercise of nine holes of golf. You can
practice archery no matter where you are, with no facilities
other than what you can tote—no bases, backboards, greens
with cups, nets, playing fields, or opponents. I know one
traveling salesman who carries his equipment with him in
his car trunk. Every evening after he has completed his sales
rounds he sets up his target in any available space around
the motel yard and shoots till dark. (He's made a lot of con-
verts in the past few years.) Another acquaintance has a
miniature archery range in his attic. He goes upstairs to
shoot a few rounds whenever he can't sleep. Doesn't cure his
insomnia, but it's better than just lying there.

Archery can be as simple or as complicated as you like
after you buy the basic outfit—bow and arrows, a quiver, a
target, and guards for your finger and arm. The expense? It
varies tremendously. A satisfactory archery set for an adult
can run anywhere from just a few dollars to a couple of
hundred. The nice thing is that once you get your basic
equipment, you're set. Your bow will last you for years, and
if you're an excellent shot—if you hit the target instead of
rocks in the background—so will your arrows.

If you're the kind who likes to fool with gadgets, archery
offers an impressive variety—from complicated range-finding
and telescopic sights to elaborate equipment for testing the
springiness of arrows. The home craftsman can do-it-himself
with projects ranging from repairing damaged arrows to con-

structing crossbows. And if he wants to go into specialized archery power tools, mail-order catalogs offer these, too.

Archery today is divided into two broad wings: "target" and "field." Both can be participated in by all members of the family. *Target archery*—a poor name, since field archers also use targets—is what most non-archers think of when they hear about shooting a bow: a whole line of people trying to hit a parallel line of targets. This is the classic method, still dominant in Europe. At this time only about a quarter of American archery enthusiasts belong to the target group.

Field archery is shooting over a varied trail resembling a golf course laid out in the deep woods. Field archers claim they are practicing for the hunt—and sure enough, some do go hunting—and fishing. A few even bring home something other than mosquito bites and poison ivy. Field archery is strictly American, but presently is being exported to northern Europe—to the Scandinavian countries and Germany.

Usually an archer is either a target man or a field archer, but not both. There are, however, a good number of archers who combine the two aspects of the sport. One, for example, is Joe Thornton, a Cherokee Indian from Oklahoma, who started as an "instinctive" field archer (one using no sighting aid) and then switched to a bow sight and target work. He became so proficient that he was sent to Oslo for the Archery world championships in 1962, and at forty-seven found himself with the first prize under his arm and the phrase "Champion of the World" tacked up after his name. He set a new record—the old one was held by an American, as usual—and beat his nearest competitor, a Finn, by 125 points.

"I originally became an archer because I like to hunt," he said after the tournament, "and the bow seemed a very good way to do it. After shooting my first tournament, I found that I liked the competition. Archery has given me some of the greatest thrills of my life, and I suppose I'll be an archer as long as I can pull a bow."

And that's the whole danger with all this bow-and-arrow foolishness. Once bitten, no true archer ever will give up the sport—not while he can still draw the string. For it takes a lot of looking to find something that gives quite the thrill you get as your string whizzes away from your ear, and your arrow, in a long, looping parabola, plunges home.

Chapter 2

LOOKING BACKWARD

A NUMBER of authorities, the stately *Encyclopaedia Britannica* for one, claim that the three most important events in the history of man were the development of speech, the discovery and application of fire, and the invention of the bow and arrow. Speech was the most important. With speech early man could tell his neighbor that striking two *particular* kinds of rock together would produce a spark. With that spark odd and marvelous things could be done. Its application enabled caveman to rise above the apes.

Without the bow, however, this early struggling rather pitiful man might not have survived.

Steps leading to the invention of the bow necessarily are speculative, but the possibilities aren't too hard to imagine. After early man learned to throw a rock—a development of momentous importance in itself—he stuck it into the split end of a stick, and made himself a spear. (Stone spear points are commonly found around ancient campsites.) The next step probably was the addition of a throwing sling—something like David's slingshot—to increase the spear's cast.

Then came the crucial step: Man made himself a bow to shoot the spear. In his *History of Archery*, Edmund Burke suggests that the bow may have evolved from a rudimentary musical instrument. (African Bushmen still use hunting bows to make music.) Ancient man was bored one day, and

17

to amuse himself he absent-mindedly strung a leather thong between the two ends of a springy stick. He pulled on the thong, let go, and it went "plunk." Another pull, another plunk. (In another few eons the addition of frets will have changed that plunk to plink, plank, plunk.) Soon his finger became sore, so to ease the work and still get those gloriously melodic plunks, he used a stick. This worked fine until he got careless, let the stick slip from his finger, and off it sailed across the cave. This genius of a caveman then logically substituted his spear for that plucking stick. Lo and behold —a bow and arrow. Man's first successful attempt to store energy.

When? That's harder to answer than "How?" Archaeologists are not at all in accord, but the barest minimum seems to be 25 thousand years ago, more probably 50, and perhaps as much as 150 thousand years. We know for sure that bows were in use 25 to 30 thousand years ago; Palaeolithic carvings of bowmen found in caves at Castellon, Spain, and elsewhere picture them.

Another item of proof: Folsom man. He roamed southwestern North America some 25 thousand years ago, and one of his arrowheads was found lodged in the bone of a species of long-extinct bison, dated by the geochronological method of radio-carbon. This fossil is now in the Museum of Natural History in Denver.

Some authorities say that a few tribes of Neanderthal man used bows and arrows more than a hundred thousand years ago, and that Cro-Magnon man depended heavily on the implement. But this view is not universally accepted.

From the *how* and *when* bows were invented to the question of *where*. The answer, with only a couple of exceptions: *everywhere*, at one time or another. Natives of the East and West Indies depended on bows. So did the Eskimos and nearly all African tribes. The ancient Egyptians fought with the bow, as did their contemporaries, the old Shang Kingdom Chinese. The Bible says that the Israelites were excel-

Paleolithic painting from a Spanish cave near the town of Albocacer, Castellon, shows early man hunting with bows and arrows.

American Museum of Natural History painting of Neolithic times by Charles R. Knight. Note the primitive bow and arrows held by second man from right.

lent archers. And so were the Greeks and Persians, not to mention the Babylonians, the Assyrians, and the legions of Caesar. (The best defense, according to invading Mongol hordes, was silken clothes; the silk entered the wound with the arrowhead, making extraction less difficult and infection less likely.)

The only notable exception to the many users of bows are the Australian aborigines. But when the rest of the world discovered them, the aborigines still were in the Stone Age. Perhaps if left on their own they eventually would have discovered the principles of archery.

The world still has a number of societies in which the bow is important. Pan American World Airways pilots claim that if they fly too low over unsettled South and Central American regions they'll be shot at by local Indians. In 1958, according to a press release issued by Pan American, an oil company engineer, while landing in a helicopter in a remote section of Bolivia, was transfixed with an eight-foot arrow. *Companions who killed two of the Indians in the ambush reported the arrow had been propelled by a 12-foot bow with a pull estimated at 250 to 400 pounds,* the statement added.

In Africa today the bow is used extensively by Bushmen and Pygmies. Pygmy bows typically are about two feet long and shoot arrows of 14 to 20 inches. Though these shafts rarely penetrate more than an inch or so, when they do strike an animal poisoned points ensure a kill. The formula for arrow-tip poison varies from tribe to tribe, but ordinarily it is a combination of saps of toxic leaves, roots, and bark, along with poison from snakes and ground-up lethal spiders. The mixture is boiled until it becomes thick and highly viscous, then it is smeared onto sharpened arrow shafts.

African Bushmen also use poison, but not so extensively and not so strong as the Pygmies'. Because Bushmen are quite muscular, they can pull heavy bows which in turn shoot large arrows at high speeds, penetrating animals deep

Congo Pygmy prepares to draw an arrow tipped with poison so toxic a nick means certain death.

Courtesy, Africa Advisory Services

enough to pierce vital organs. Rather than having to rely on poison, Bushmen arrows kill by hemorrhage.

In both equipment and hunting technique, the Bushmen's archery is singularly similar to that of our Neolithic ancestors. The bows usually are made from cane, the arrows from two different woods: the shaft is of springy, tough reed and the point is of fire-hardened hardwood. The point is quite long—three inches or so—and breaks off easily. This way if an animal gets away, he'll probably carry off only the point of an arrow.

Another Neolithic-like archer, famous for his prowess, was the American Indian. Sadly, his fame is undeserved. Though the Red Man used his bow daily in search of food, and though every tribe from coast to coast relied on archery for its existence, the Indian just wasn't a good shot. This wasn't his fault, really; it was his equipment. Terrible. He made up for wavering arrow flight, however, by being an excellent hunter—perhaps as good as the world ever has known. And this ability to sneak up to within a few feet of an animal made all the difference.

In Europe, bows and arrows were used more or less throughout recorded history. Interestingly enough, archery technology advanced little until about A.D. 1300; a bow from the year 100 could hardly be told from another fabricated in the year 1250.

Use of archery as a major instrument of war came rather late in European history. The first massive success, in fact, wasn't until the Battle of Hastings in 1066. William, Duke of Normandy, crossed the Channel, landed in England with thousands of fellow Normans, whaled the tar out of King Harold, and forevermore was called William the Conqueror. The victorious William was crowned King of England on Christmas Day, 1066, and that was that.

One reason William's followers did such a good job was that the Danes were always great archers, and the Normans, who fought for William, were descendants of these Danes. (Norman is just a sloppy way of saying Northman, or Norseman.) These fine Danish archers put their passed-down knowledge to use, and it was this, say many historians, that turned the tide in William's favor. (The shooting of an arrow through the eye of King Harold during the battle helped, too.)

Use of archery in war slowly grew until 1300 or so, when just about everyone who was anyone in conquering circles was relying either on the standard short bow or the newly developed crossbow. (More about that in the Chapter on Crossbows.) In the meantime, however, interesting things were happening in South Wales, of all places. There, the now-famous longbow was being perfected, an instrument six feet long that shot 36-inch arrows heavy enough to pierce armor. So formidable were the Welsh longbows that the English reluctantly gave up their old-fashioned short bow and took up the longbow instead.

And it was a good thing they did, for otherwise, today's

archery historians couldn't call August 26, 1346, "archery's greatest day"—the day the famous Battle of Crécy was fought.

As usual, it was the English and French mixing it up—the French under the leadership of King Philip of Valois, and the English under Edward III. Edward was in battle position first, stretching his men on an elevated line extending from the river Maye, near Crécy, to the village of Wadicourt. On the side of the English were something like 18,000 men, approximately 11,000 of whom were longbowmen.

The French army arrived in late afternoon. Just as they were moving into battle position, a wild thunderstorm broke, soaking everyone. King Philip decided to camp for the night and have a fresh fight in the morning. But he had so many men with him (estimates place the number at anywhere from 15,000 to 100,000—with perhaps 40,000 about right), that the rear end of the line didn't know what the front was doing. Instead of stopping, it kept right on marching, more or less pushing the front forward. The troops were getting out of control. So for lack of much else to do, the King of France ordered the attack.

In the forefront were some 6,000 mercenary crossbowmen from Italy. Their job was to shatter the line of English longbowmen up on the hill. Unfortunately for the crossbowmen, they had neglected to waterproof their strings and the downpour weakened them, rendering them almost useless. The British longbowmen, on the other hand, having learned to shoot in drizzly England, had their strings well waxed and waterproofed.

According to reliable reports of the battle, the Italians came yelling up the hill while the well-disciplined English silently stayed frozen in position. They waited until the crossbowmen were almost at the line, then shot on signal, sending arrows in a barrage described as "thick as snow, with a terrible noise, much like a tempestuous wind. . . ."

Shocked and badly hurt, what was left of the crossbow-

men turned and fled—right into the advancing French horse-
men and foot soldiers. The French knights were furious with
the chickenhearted Italians, and galloped right into them,
pushing them in reverse. Back up the hill came this rabble of
men and horses, using more energy in fighting each other
than in advancing.

From their safe position the English shot surely and
smoothly, with the result that most of the advancing party
died on the spot. Hastily the French consolidated their men
and charged a third time. Again they were cut down. New
troops, arriving fresh from the line of march, kept pouring
into the rear, and every time enough assembled to warrant
another rush, they rushed. At least sixteen waves of French-
men attacked the English (the Italians having given up the
whole thing before darkness), and each time more were left
on the ground than retreated.

By midnight, about 60 Englishmen had been killed. The
French army had been practically annihilated—those scores
of thousands. The longbow had been proved, and for centuries it remained *the* English weapon.

One man who waged his own limited war with his longbow had a name that has become one of the most famous in
all English history: Robin Hood. Some say that Robin Hood
was not a single person but the embodiment of a whole
series of men about whom legends grew and ballads were
sung. But as I prefer to believe that Shakespeare rather than
Bacon wrote the plays, I believe, too (yes, Virginia), that
there was a Robin Hood.

Robin Hood, it is claimed, entered this world through the
portals of Wakefield, somewhere in the thirteenth century.
He ran into trouble with the current king, fought him, then
deserted his lawful wife for fun and games in the wood with
Maid Marion, Little John and "100 tall yeomen, which were
mightie men and exceeding good archers." Wealthy earls
and priests who happened near Sherwood Forest were re-
lieved of their valuables by the Hood mob, much to the

chagrin of the Sheriff of Nottingham. And if a little extra loot was left over, the boys would toss it to the neighborhood peasants to keep them pacified.

Robin Hood met his unfortunate end at the hands of a woman named Elizabeth de Stainton. He became ill and asked Elizabeth to bleed him a bit—a practice that in those days cured most any sickness. But she treacherously overdid it, letting nearly all the blood run out. This made Robin sicker yet.

Just before he died he blew one last blast on his hunting horn, summoning Little John. Robin asked John for his bow, hauled back with his last erg of strength, let fly with an arrow through a window, and dropped dead. They buried him where the arrow struck, at the base of a giant oak tree still standing in Sherwood Forest, so they say.

The bow prospered as the major English war implement for some 300 years—even after the introduction of gunpowder—then began to decline sometime around the middle of the sixteenth century, just prior to the reign of Elizabeth I (1558–1603). Just before the bow's fall as *the* weapon, the greatest archery book of all time was published: *Toxophilus*, by Roger Ascham. (That's pronounced *askam*, not *asham*.) The publication of this little volume was tremendously important to the sport, and only an archer can appreciate the thoroughness with which Ascham describes the best way to shoot, the equipment, the philosophy behind it all. The book served archery in about the same way that Izaak Walton's writing served the sport of fishing.

When *Toxophilus* was published in 1545, Henry VIII liked it so well "he gave me a living for it," said Ascham. The amount was 10 pounds a year, quite a good sum in those days. So interested was Henry in archery that he issued a statute stating that every male from seven to sixty years old was required to own and practice with a bow. The law also required that targets be placed at strategic corners in every town so that inhabitants who carried bows around with them would be sure of having something to shoot at that wouldn't shoot back.

With a little rewriting, *Toxophilus* could very well be used as a basic text today. Ascham's steps of the shoot ("standynge, nockynge, drawynge, howldynge, lowsynge"—plus aiming, which he considered to be part of all the others) are, in fact, what almost all how-to archery books (including this one) are based upon. The word "toxophilus," incidentally, is derived from the Greek *toxon*, or bow, and *philite*, to love. Our word "toxic" stems from *toxicon*, arrow poison.

With the passing of King Henry three years after *Toxophilus* was published, perhaps the last real proponent of mass archery for war purposes was gone. That there were still staunch backers of the bow is proved, however, by the following opening portions of a sermon preached by Bishop Latimer before Henry's son and successor, Edward VI: "The arte of shutynge hath ben in tymes past much estemed in this realme [to continue in modern spelling], for it is a gift of God, that he has given us to excel all other nations. It has been God's instrument, whereby he has given us many victories against our enemies. But now we have taken up whoring in the towns, instead of shooting in the fields. A wondrous thing, that so excellent a gift of God should be so little esteemed. . . . In the reverence of God, let it be continued. Let a proclamation go forth charging the Justices of Peace that they see much acts and statutes kept as were made for the purpose [of promoting archery]."

The tirade seemed to have little effect on the swing of history, however; the bow fell into gradual disuse as gunpowder steadily encroached.

In the first few centuries of White Man's America, nobody much cared about bothering with archery, except for a few screwballs who also went for such activities as riding to the hounds and polo playing. And these folks usually had learned the rudiments in England. Archery, nonetheless, always kept a few eminent supporters. Benjamin Franklin, for example, in a letter sent to a general in the second year of the Revolutionary War, said, "I still wish, with you, that pikes could be introduced, and I would add bows and arrows; these were good weapons not wisely laid aside." He pointed out that one could shoot a bow silently, that a bow is comparatively cheap, and that it can shoot as true as a musket.

Despite Franklin's efforts, it wasn't until 1828 that archery really got going in this country. In that year four friends got together in Philadelphia to form a rather elite club called The United Bowmen, a group that still is active, and to which we owe much.

The next notable event in the history of U.S. archery was the discharge from the Confederate Army—after taking a Yankee minié ball in the chest—of Maurice Thompson. With his brother Will, also newly discharged, Maurice decided to live in the wilderness, to rest and hunt while he recovered from his wound. But the Thompsons were rebels, so guns were forbidden. As a last resort, they decided to live off the land, to hunt game with bows. For two years—1866 to 1868 —they camped in Florida's Everglades near Lake Okechobee, and in Georgia's great Okefinokee Swamp. The brothers then moved to Crawfordsville, Indiana, where they opened a law office.

But they didn't forget about archery. In 1877 Maurice's *The Witchery of Archery* was published, a rather poetic examination of the sport and a long, lyrical look at the years the brothers spent in the wilderness. The book was an instant success, and its impact could be seen across the nation in the hundreds of clubs that sprang up overnight. When the National Archery Association was formed on January 23, 1879, Crawfordsville became its headquarters, Maurice its first president. Brother Will won a number of championships during the following years, the last time in 1908 at the age of sixty-two.

The next great archery exponent was Dr. Saxton Pope,

who, with his hunting partner Art Young, brought before the American public the fact that the bow can be a vital hunting weapon. He did it principally through his widely reported hunting trips to Africa.

Today, however, Dr. Pope perhaps is best known through Ishi, the last wild American Indian. Ishi had belonged to the little-known Yana tribe, a band that in 1872 was nearly wiped out in battle. The few survivors, diseased and homeless, wandered the wilderness and died one by one until only a single descendant remained—Ishi. Half starved and crazed, he was discovered in 1911 hiding in the corral of a slaughterhouse near Oroville, California. He was promptly labeled a wildman and thrown into jail. Finally he was identified as a Yana and brought to the University of California. He spent the rest of his life (he died in 1916) under the care and protection of the staff of the University's Museum of Anthropology. Dr. Pope became Ishi's personal physician as well as his good friend, and from him learned an immense amount about native Indian lore, particularly in regard to bowhunting.

Dr. Pope also ran extensive experiments with native archery equipment and established specifications regarding accuracy, penetrating power, strength, etc., for bows and arrows of a variety of old cultures. Here, for example, are a few samples of Dr. Pope's "Conclusions," published in *Bows and Arrows:*

The greatest flight shot achieved by any aboriginal bow at our disposal is 210 yards. . . .

The striking force of a 50-pound bow with a one-ounce arrow at 10 feet is 20 foot pounds. . . .

The red wood of the yew has more cast than the white wood. . . .

A Tarter bow, though the most powerful to draw, is a failure as a weapon to shoot. . . .

A bodkin-pointed arrow, shot from a heavy bow, can penetrate steel mail.

With the publicity given to the hunting exploits of Dr. Pope and Art Young, American hunters began to take archery a little more seriously. Such writers as Dr. Robert Elmer, one-time NAA Champion, kept alive and bubbling the excitement of target archery. (Dr. Elmer wrote *Archery* and *Target Archery*.) But it took the flamboyant and often astonishing Howard Hill to show the public what good shooting is really like. Through his movies, public demonstrations, writings, and instruction Hill has exposed more people to the beauty and thrill of archery than anyone else in history.

Hill's publicizing the sport, however, is not the main reason for the present upsurge in archery interest, it is a direct outgrowth of two movements begun in the 1930's. One was a change in equipment; the other, an evolution in its use.

Change in use came with the general movement away from conventional target shooting to field work (discussed in detail in Chapter 13)—the gradual switchover from archery of fixed distances over level ground to that in which targets are set at a variety of unknown distances over changing terrain.

The other revolution came when physicists and engineers became interested, in the year just before and after World War II, in the mechanics of the bow and arrow. They found out for the first time how bows and arrows actually operate, and the suggestions they evolved for improvement actually worked.

The initial research largely was pioneered by physicist Clarence N. Hickman—first in the research laboratory of the American Piano Company, then at the Bell Telephone Laboratories. (He was involved with magnetic recording at Bell Labs, and during World War II worked on rockets with the National Defense Research Committee; all told, securing some 125 patents.) The applications of Dr. Hickman's theories on the physics of the bow and arrow were in the main proved by Dr. Paul E. Klopsteg, president of Chicago's

Central Scientific Company. As a direct result of the research, bow efficiency increased from 60 percent to 90 percent.

Then, with the advent of fiberglass, the whole archery industry exploded with vigor. One result is that the bow and arrow have changed more in the past 25 years than in all the 50 thousand years of previous history. Another is that American equipment is today, by far, the best in the world. And American archers have made winning international championships habitual.

Fact is, any good high school archer today—given modern equipment and training—could shoot rings around King Edward III's best men, and if Robin Hood showed up at any decent meet with his old bow, he'd be lucky even to qualify.

Chapter 3

THE RIGHT BOW —
HOW TO FIND IT

A SHORT time ago I was talking with an old friend, a six-foot-two, 220-pound ex-football player. He's a great guy with a gun—can snip the tip from a cigarette at 30 paces —and there's nothing he likes better than to hop in a canoe for a week's paddling through the wilderness. A real sportsman.

Thinking he might have some good stories to tell, I asked him if he ever hunted with a bow. He shrugged and rather apologetically said, "No, I don't. I tried archery years ago, but to be honest I guess I'm just not man enough. I borrowed a set for a couple of weeks from an archer I know— just to see how I'd do. I could hardly pull the arrow back, and when I did, the darn thing wouldn't hold steady. I didn't hit the target at all, much less the bull's-eye. Was a darn good bow, too—seventy pound pull."

Seventy pounds. That told the story—and the sad tale illustrates the most important consideration when first trying your hand at archery: Use a bow you can handle.

Equipment manufacturers across the country spend thousands of dollars each year telling the amateur to be sure to start with the right tackle (equipment). But likely as not, the average beginner walks into the nearest department store, eyes the sports counter equipment, studiously examines a couple of bows, then lets the clerk (whose specialty might be badminton) decide which outfit he should buy. The would-be archer walks out with a bow too short, a dozen pounds too heavy, and made of the wrong material for his needs. The new arrows are likely to be designed for someone with an entirely different build. At home, the amateur can't hit a thing, ends up with a sore arm and a grudge against the sport. Another potential bowman lost.

In the long history of archery, craftsmen have had plenty of time to develop tackle. Manufacturers in the United States—and to a lesser extent, England and Sweden—have learned to mass-produce equipment better than any Robin Hood ever laid eyes on. But unlike firearms, bows have no built-in accuracy; bull's-eye-hitting comes only with long practice, solid instruction, and strong will. So even if you buy *the* perfect set for you, you'll not become a marksman immediately; and if you get the wrong tackle for you, chances are you'll not become a marksman at all. Your interest won't last that long.

O.K. Then how *do* you go about buying your first bow?

First off, get a general idea of what's available. Pick up an archery or general sports magazine (some are listed at the end of this book) and send away for catalogs. You can buy by mail, but ordinarily it's best to try out the equipment, to examine various bows, get the feel of them, test them before you lay down your money. Though nicely packaged archery sets are available, it's best to buy your bows, arrows and accessories individually, for each must fit you personally.

If there's an archery society nearby, hang around the clubhouse for a while. Let the members know you're interested in learning about the sport. They'll spend hours (if you let them) enthusiastically giving you pointers on tackle and technique. You probably won't even have to ask questions.

They also may recommend a store run by an experienced archer known for his fairness and reliability. And maybe one of the top men in the club will accompany you when you shop. Nothing better than to have an expert along—mainly because rare is the salesman in a general sports store who knows a fistmele from a fistula.

In general, a bow-buyer should consider five characteristics: weight, construction and material, shape, length, and price.

WEIGHT: This is the "pull," the force in pounds necessary to get a 28-inch arrow back full length in the bow. It's in the weight area that many amateurs go wrong; they figure they're stronger (or should be) than they are. It's like learning to pole vault. You don't start trying for 16 feet; you begin low, then when technique is developed, move the bar up.

To find the weight for you, test the bows in the shop's racks till you find one you can draw easily, then select one five pounds heavier. If you are a beginner, draw the bow only under the supervision of a salesman. With an arrow in place, draw it *all the way back* and sight across the arrow point. (A bow always is shot at full draw.) If it starts wavering in 10 or 12 seconds, it's about right. If you can't hold it fully drawn more than six seconds without a fight, it's too heavy; drop five pounds or so. If you're doubtful, lean toward the light side.

Generally, pre-teen-agers can handle bow strengths up to 20 pounds or so. Most women and teen-age boys can start with a bow of 20 to 25 pounds. Men ordinarily begin with one of 30 to 40 pounds pull and often work up to 45 or 50 pounds or higher for hunting.

The beginner should have a bow light enough to shoot for hours at a stretch without tiring. To become a sharpshooter, you have to concentrate on form, not be distracted with hauling back excess weight all afternoon. When you learn to pepper the bull's-eye consistently with your lightweight bow —when you fit, draw, aim, and release without even thinking —then you can consider heavier equipment. Not before.

Maybe you'll stay with the light bow. Some do. Most

hot-shot tournament archers, for example, use weights no higher than about 40 pounds—so they can shoot for long periods while maintaining accuracy. Marie Stotts, 1962 National Field Archery Association champion, used a 32-pound bow to capture the title. Hunters, on the other hand, often use bows of 60 pounds and up. They expect to shoot only now and then—and make each arrow count. In fact, some states require bows of at least 45 pounds for hunting.

CONSTRUCTION AND MATERIAL: Until after World War II almost all fine bows were made of a single slab of wood. These are called "self" bows, and a few archers still claim that they are best—provided they're of top grade.

Woods in present-day self bows are mostly osage orange or lemonwood, occasionally yew or hickory. Lemonwood (it isn't lemon at all, but tropical hardwood) is often the cheapest, and for the young beginner, quite satisfactory. But the accuracy of a lemonwood bow is not the best; sooner or later, you'll probably be dissatisfied with it. Hickory is a little better, osage orange and yew considerably so.

Most of today's wooden self bows actually are made from two pieces spliced together. It's easier to make both arms of the same quality that way. A few are available, however, made from a single piece. One kind of self bow imported from Japan (and a few of this type are made in the U.S.) is the seven- or nine-ply bamboo. It's light, cheap, fairly accurate, but hard to find.

You occasionally see bows of solid metal—steel, aluminum, even magnesium—but not very often any more. They tend to "kick" in the hand, making accuracy doubtful. And though they're long-lasting, consistent, and may even be disassembled for easy carrying, they're often heavy and less comfortable to shoot.

The same general drawbacks may be said of solid fiberglass bows, but because they are very cheap and virtually indestructible, they're pretty good for youngsters, for beginning archery classes, and for that first feel of shooting. No sense forking over half a hundred bucks or so until you're sure your child is going to be interested. (There's even a model, made by Stemmler Archery of Manorville, N.Y., actually selling for only $1.95. You can hardly steal one for that.)

By far the most popular bows today are the laminates, for use both by the amateur and the champion. With few exceptions the modern bow consists of a core of tapered hardwood, bonded front and back, like a sandwich, with continuous-strand fiberglass. The glass strengthens the sturdy center against breakage and fatigue, or loss of springiness. The core usually is of select, straight-grained northern hard maple, sometimes sub-laminated with American walnut, white holly, purple heart, or osage. So far no one has proved whether or not these other woods add anything to the maple in cast or accuracy. But they do add visual appeal.

Speaking of things decorative, some bow handles—with intricate inlays and laminations—truly are works of art. And indications are that some manufacturers spend as much time and money designing beautiful handles as they do engineering the mechanical aspects. Black walnut, northern hard maple, and American walnut are common, while such woods as white holly, rosewood, purple heart, bird's-eye maple, and zebra wood are sometimes used for startling contrast. One bow maker—Birnie Bows of Dallas—uses a total of 95 separate pieces of wood in the handle of one of its models, reflected in the $100 price tag.

"Black Watch" by Birnie Bows shows the beauty possible with artful blending of hardwoods. Working limbs are of maple and purple heart, faced and backed with fiberglass; handle section is laminated with bird's-eye maple, African walnut, and other woods.

SHAPE: Time was—and not so long ago either—when nearly all bows were *straight*. Today, an estimated 90 percent (not including those packed away in attics) are of the *recurve* type. A conventional straight bow is just that—when unstrung, it has no curves at all. An unstrung recurved bow, on the other hand, is more or less straight to about a half-foot from the ends, then curves sharply out, away from the shooter. When strung, the straight bow forms a simple curve, a quarter-moon shape. The recurve, on the other hand, is easily spotted by its two miniature reversed Cupid bows at the ends that "unwind" as the bow is drawn.

When a straight bow is released, the string speeds forward rather evenly until the bow is in its undrawn position. When a recurve bow of the "working" type is released, the two little end bows relax first, pulling the string forward, then the main bow relaxes, giving the arrow a little extra zing at the last moment. (The process is discussed in detail in Chapter 11.) Big advantages are two: The bow is more smoothly drawn, and it gives a smarter *cast*, archers' term for power. A modern recurve bow of 30-pound draw probably gives a better cast than the best of the American Indian's 75-pound straight bows, and almost any recurve will give a minimum of 15 percent more power than the same weight straight bow.

This style bow is referred to as a *working* recurve, to differentiate it from the *static* recurve, the tips of which do not unbend. The purpose of static recurve tips is simply to lengthen the bow so that the draw is easier. Rarely are true static recurves seen today (the bow looks as though the tips were sharply broken), but there are a number of *modified* recurves around, those which unwind only part way.

Good as recurved bows are, they present a few problems. In the first place a recurve is tougher to make than a straight bow, therefore costs more. Second, this type is difficult to string; more physical strength is needed and the limbs can more easily be twisted out of line. Third, a recurve bow magnifies shooting mistakes.

Now, add one more factor to the shape of either type bow: the angle, if any, at which the two limbs leave the handle. If the bow's limbs bend "backwards" when the string is removed—if the limbs bend *away* from the archer—the bow is called a *reflex*. If the handle is set somewhat forward of the limbs or if the limbs tend to bend in toward the archer, it is a *deflexed* bow.

Reflexed bows usually are straight bows, and when strung, the bow bends back around, against its natural curvature. When a straight bow is strung, you can't tell whether it's reflexed or not. Most modern recurved bows are deflexed, and the reason is that this design places the bow hand farther in front of the action and gives everything more stability.

Which style, straight or recurve, should you buy? If you're a good shot and expect to keep up your practice, a recurve is probably the bow for you. If your bow will sit untouched in the storeroom for weeks, and if you expect primarily to do occasional shooting, your best bet is a straight bow, or one moderately recurved.

For hunting, most people find the recurved bow best; cast is important in the hunt, and recurved bows are just more powerful than straight ones. A few hunters, however, feel that the higher accuracy of the straight bow more than makes up for its lack of power. When someone asked Hollywood's Howard Hill (probably best known of American bowmen and owner of an atticful of trophies) why he doesn't use a recurved bow, he answered, "I'm just not skilled enough to shoot one accurately."

Hill probably was talking about the bows of the early and mid 1950's, however. Today's designs are better, the fiberglass is more uniform, the general bow is more stable. There still is a difference, but not enough to get excited about.

Far more recurved bows are sold today than straight. The

STRAIGHT OR SEMI-RECURVED BOW

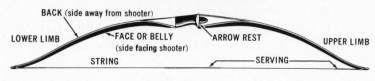

RECURVED BOW

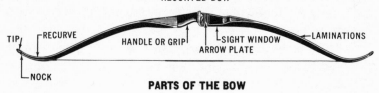

PARTS OF THE BOW

reason may be as much psychological as mechanical. Recurve bows are fancier and appear more expensive, while straight bows seem plain in comparison, almost old-fashioned.

* A bow's handle is the center section that doesn't bend. Also called the riser, it includes the grip, the overdraw, the arrow rest and the sight window. The *grip* is the section you grab, contoured to fit the hand. Grips are designed to position the bow correctly, and to more or less force the archer into holding only one way—so that he doesn't inadvertently change his hand position from time to time. The only criterion here applicable to the beginner is comfort. Get a bow with a grip that feels like it fits.

The *overdraw* is the section that projects above your bow hand. On top of this shelf is the *arrow rest*. This gets the arrow away from resting on the shooting hand, and assures the archer that the end of the arrow is positioned the same with each shot. Usually the arrow sits on something other than the bare shelf wood—a tuft of stiff bristles, a few cemented-on feathers, a molded hunk of plastic. A small piece of soft leather ordinarily is glued to the bow to cut down on arrow-slap noise.

Just above the arrow rest a large slab of the bow is cut away. This is the *sight window,* and its purpose is twofold: It lets the archer see where he's aiming, and allows the arrow to move in closer to the center of the bow. Nothing much to look for here when you're buying, except to be sure that if you're right-handed, you get a right-handed bow—with the sight window on the left.

The longer the handle the faster the bow, but the more difficult to draw. That's because with a long handle there's not so much *length* of limbs to bend.

LENGTH: Conventional bows vary from about four to six feet. Generally speaking, a shorter bow is better for hunting, a longer one for target work. The main difference is that a short bow is easier to handle in the woods, is lighter, and shoots faster because it bends more. (However, a long bow with a long, unbendable handle riser may also shoot fast.) Unfortunately, a short bow exaggerates errors—just when you want every arrow to find its mark. Another disadvantage: Because of the shorter string, the bend angle at the draw point of the string sometimes pinches fingers. One more: Because it is under higher stress, a short bow usually has a shorter life.

A long bow has smoother action, is more accurate. Before modern materials were available, in fact, the long bow was the only one with any accuracy at all. But because of its length, it's a problem in the woods. If you get a maximum length bow, don't plan to do much deep-forest hunting.

Now then, which length for you? First, better not look at one under five feet or so. A general rule for an all-purpose bow is to start with one that, when unstrung, is four or five inches shorter than you are. If you know you will use it mainly for hunting, get one still a little shorter; if exclusively for target shooting, a little longer. If in doubt, edge toward longness.

Incidentally, when once you pick a bow length, stick to it

until you've become a master. Shifting back and forth from long to short will only stretch out your training period.

PRICE: Bows come in an astonishing range of prices, anywhere from a couple of dollars for so-so dime-store models to a hundred dollars or more—much more. Generally, a fairly good bow will cost somewhere between $35 and $65. One archer suggests getting a relatively poor bow for around $10 or $15 and plan to give it to a neighbor as soon as it's mastered. This probably is a poor idea. A jerky bow (one big fault of cheap ones) will often quickly put the damper on any prospective bowmanship. (On the other hand, in 1951, a Pennsylvania woman paid $12 for a "child's" lemonwood bow and killed a deer with it the following month.) Better idea is to pay a little more—at least $25 or $30—and save up for a really good one later on, when you'll know more about the style and weight you want. Some economy at the outset will let you splurge later on, but don't overdo the thrift routine. By the time you buy your second bow, you should have settled on a design you'll stick with for years.

All reputable manufacturers, by the way, give guarantees with their equipment—usually from one to three years.

Other things to look for when shopping:

. . . Make sure the drawn bow bends evenly from handle to tips.

. . . Check to see that the string divides the bow in half along the entire length. Do this by leaning one end on the floor in front of you and sighting down the string. If it doesn't divide the bow, the bow is warped or twisted. Reject it.

. . . Beware of bows made by companies not nationally known.

. . . Note the grain in self bows; the best are of straight-grained wood.

. . . With your thumbnail, try to scrape off the finish. If anything more than wax comes off, better move on. Think of how the finish will look after a few trips through dense woods.

. . . Look closely at knots. They should either be plugged or have extra wood left around them. Look for a neat, solid job in either case. It's best, of course, if there are no knots at all.

. . . Generally, a recurve bow with medium wide limbs will be more stable, less sensitive, than one with narrow limbs, though a small amount of cast may be lost.

. . . Don't expect to be able to *buy* high scores.

If you merely want to try out the sport to see if you like it, you might spend a few nights at a commercial roadside range with rented or borrowed equipment. But be sure you use good tackle, including a bow that's not too heavy and arrows not too worn. You might even consider buying a used bow. An experienced archer can tell in a single outing if it's a good buy.

Most good sports shops either have their own backyard range or will let you borrow a bow for home testing. When you do test, it's a good idea if an experienced bowman tries out the outfit with you. He'll be able to judge such things as consistency, smooth cast and "feel in the hand"; things a beginner can't tell too much about. He'll also be better able to tell if the bow "stacks"; if it draws unevenly—a fault that should eliminate it from consideration immediately. A properly designed bow has a pull that is uniform throughout the draw, while a stacked bow of 45 pounds, for example, may take up 30 pounds in the first 24 inches, and 15 in the last 4—and that's bad. Incidentally, if you borrow a new bow for testing, put a strip of tape over the arrow rest before shooting—so the bow will still be new if returned.

One more thing: Be sure to do your testing with properly matched arrows. The smoothest bow in the world won't seem any good otherwise.

Chapter 4

ABOUT: ARROWS

TWO archers, one an old hand, the other a beginner, were out shooting one day not so long ago in upstate New York. The beginner seemed to have learned his early lessons well. His technique was consistent, his release smooth, his form flawless. One trouble: His arrows were scattered all over the place—no grouping on the target at all. The experienced bowman inspected his friend's bow, and satisfied, gave it back. Then he went over each of the arrows.

"Your bow is fine," he said, "but these arrows are terrible. They're warped, the points are on crooked, and the fletching is askew. You couldn't hit a buffalo at ten paces. Here, let's try an experiment."

The old bowman cut down a fairly straight sapling, notched the ends, and fitted on a string. He shot a few practice arrows to get the feel of the makeshift bow, then taking his own aluminum arrows, placed the full set in a basketball-size circle at 25 yards. (The bow probably wouldn't have held up for an hour, but for the lesson, it lasted long enough.)

Then he picked up his own bow—an old and trusted weapon proved over the years—and shot his friend's set of arrows. Of the six, only two hit the circle; the rest didn't even come close.

"A good man can shoot with a bad bow," he explained, "but no one can hit consistently unless he uses matched arrows."

The key word here is "matched." It means that all arrows in a set are straight and perfectly round, that they're of the same material, weight, length and spine (stiffness), that they're fletched (feathered) alike with identical balance points. No set is perfect. But if the arrows aren't at least close, they're unmatched and, therefore, nearly worthless.

A set of matched arrows costs half again as much as a run-of-the-mill batch—and well they should. Finding needles in haystacks is no tougher than picking out a set of matched dowels. Strength, elasticity, and weight of wood depend on the cellular density and distribution of sap, and because the thickness of annual growth rings varies with the growing season, even a difference of a half inch in a wood billet can produce a marked change in density.

The only way to match wooden arrows is by grouping. Manufacturers shape dowels by the thousands, group them in piles by weight (usually within five grains), then subdivide by stiffness, allowing a 2 percent tolerance. Take a pile of 500 choice dowels cut from the same log, and you'll probably find that when you've sorted them into matched bunches, no batch will contain more than 30.

Roughly, arrows are divided into: practice, target, field, hunting, fishing, and flight.

Practice arrows are cut-rate, unmatched wooden missiles, worth the money to only the rawest beginner, and perhaps not even to him. If you are just starting out, your first half-dozen arrows will vanish pretty fast, mainly through breakage and loss. So it's O.K. to pick up six practice arrows to learn rudiments of technique. But as soon as these are used up, it's a good rule to avoid buying unmatched arrows from then on.

Target arrows have small points and relatively small feathers. Designed for target work, in a pinch they can be shot on field ranges—but they'll quickly wear.

Field arrows—used mainly for practice on cross-country field courses—are heavier and more rugged than target arrows. The points are bulkier—corresponding to the weights of hunting points. Feathers must be longer in order to control them. Field arrows also may be used on the target range.

Hunting arrows are similar to field arrows—sturdy shaft with long feathers—except that the point means business.

Fishing arrows have barbed or hunting-type heads, often with hinged barbs that open inside the fish. Metal or fiberglass shafts are more common (wood absorbs water), and because ballistics is of little concern at close range, fishing arrows may have no fletching at all—the line dragging behind keeps the point forward. If vanes are used, they're made of waterproof plastic or rubber.

Flight arrows are for one thing only: distance, with no thought of target hitting. (See Chapter 15.) They have small vanes—usually of plastic—with correspondingly small points, are of the most select stock, and are finished smooth as oil.

When buying arrows—of whatever kind—make sure they are the correct length. If you are an African Pygmy, your arrow need be only a sharpened stick weighing about 80 grains; if you had been an Olde Englishman, your arrow could be a yard long. But more likely, your arrow length will fall somewhere around 2¼ feet, the exact size depending on your arm length, and consequently your draw distance. Target-arrow length is measured from the bottom of the nock (where the string fits) to the base (or shoulder) of the point. Hunting arrows are measured about ¾ of an inch back from the broadhead base—insurance against finger slicing if overdrawn slightly.

If you already have a bow, simply substitute a yardstick for the arrow to find the right length for you. Measure from the bow's belly—the part nearest you. If you haven't purchased your bow, measure between your fingertips with your arms outstretched, then check this table:

Spread Measurement	Arrow Length
57–59"	22–23"
60–62"	23–24"
63–65"	24–25"
66–68"	25–26"
69–71"	26–27"
72–74"	27–28"
75–77"	28–29"
More than 77"	30"

If you are buying your first arrows, get them about an inch longer than you think necessary; your draw probably will increase a bit as your muscles get used to the idea.

Test for arrow length when a tape isn't handy (in the field, for instance) by placing the nock in the center of your chest and extending both arms forward, palms inward. Your fingertips should reach about halfway up the shank of a target point, or to about the base of a field point, or ¾ of an inch below a hunting or fishing point.

And if you get the wrong length arrow? A couple of things might happen—both nasty. If your arrow is too long, you may automatically draw to its full length; the unaccustomed overdrawing can snap the string, and pow! there goes your bow; the pent-up energy and sudden release can shatter it as it throws itself forward and bends backwards. If the arrow is too short, the point may slip over so it snags in the belly of the bow; all the force will be directed into shattering the arrow, a splinter of which can slice through your hand. Another thing: If you aim by noting the arrow point in relation to your target, your distance will be thrown off by the wrong-length arrow's point resting an unaccustomed distance from your eye.

By the way, here's an interesting sidelight to the relationship between arrow length and bow weight. Bow weight is based on a 28-inch draw. An average bow of 50 pounds will change its pulling weight about 2½ pounds for each inch of draw over or under 28 inches. Thus, if your draw is 30 inches, your 50-pound bow actually will weigh 55 pounds.

So far as arrow shaft material is concerned, today's archer has the choice of wood, fiberglass, and aluminum. Each has its proponents, each its detractors. One drawback to glass and aluminum arrows is that in many states they are illegal for hunting. Reason: a wounded animal can snap off a wooden arrow on trees; fiberglass and metal won't break.

Fiberglass arrows

The newest material for arrows, fiberglass, is still more or less in the experimental stage. Some well-known champions, however, use nothing else, and the time is quickly approaching when fiberglass will be the most popular shafting for general use. Glass arrows have much to recommend them. For one thing, they're impervious to water—no warping from high humidity or from lake dunkings. Fiberglass arrows may rupture or crush from glancing off rocks, or break if bent to extremes, but they will never permanently bend. Many will spring back into shape after being nearly bent double.

Another advantage to glass arrows is their uniformity. Machines grind them out sausage-like, all of the same density, stiffness, diameter, weight. Matching is automatic.

On the other hand, many glass arrows are heavy, requiring high trajectories, and with field and hunting shafts the five-degree-tapered forward ends are often much too short to reach to the bottom of standard arrowhead sockets, putting excessive strain on the arrowhead and the cement used to attach it.

They're much more expensive than comparable wooden arrows, too. With increased usage and mass production, however, fiberglass-arrow cost will undoubtedly drop, and when it does, don't be surprised if wooden arrows are relegated to the toy box.

Aluminum arrows

Aluminum also is making serious inroads on wood. Fact is, nearly every national and international target and field tournament over the past decade or two has been won by an archer shooting lightweight aluminum shafts. The secret again is uniformity—in strength, spine and straightness. Like those of fiberglass, seamless metal arrows can be turned out by machine in nearly identical batches. Another big advantage of aluminum arrows is flat trajectory, resulting from their light weight. The difference in cast between an average aluminum and fiberglass missile is about 5 yards at healthy distances. In other words, if you are using a bow sight calibrated for fiberglass, and your target is 80 yards away, you set the sight at 75 when you switch to aluminum. Doesn't seem like much to the amateur, but when an old bowman first looses an aluminum shaft, the difference in feel is staggering.

A set of aluminum arrows is a must for every experienced target bowman, even though the cost is high. But they're not for amateurs. "We don't recommend their purchase where arrow loss is common," says Kittredge Bow Hut of South Pasadena, California, one of the country's largest mail-order houses, "nor where misses will cause serious bending of the shafts. . . . These are not arrows for the rank beginner."

Most of today's aluminum arrows come from Jas. D. Easton, Inc., Van Nuys, California, where a 10,000-square-foot plant is devoted exclusively to extruding identically uniform arrow shafts. The company has been marketing aluminum since right after World War II, and has developed an extremely strong alloy (coded 24SRT-X) that tests at over 90,000 psi—more than double the strength of mild steel,

considering the weight factor. In 1948, says President Doug
Easton, an order for 100 shafts was considered a large one.
Today, orders for 10- or 20-thousand are not uncommon.

Since 1958 all Easton shafts have been sandblast etched
with the trademark and shaft size code, a code that stands
for exactly the same thing as it did in 1958—which means
that if you bought a dozen arrows then and lost a couple in
the interim, you can replace the missing shafts today and be
sure they'll fly the same. Weights for particular sizes have
not changed since 1946. (A slightly different alloy, trade-
marked XX75, recently was placed on the market. It is similar to 24SRT-X, but has a strength of up to 101,000 psi, is
one percent heavier, and slightly less springy.)

Aluminum arrows vary from a shaft diameter of 7/32nds
of an inch and a wall thickness of .016 inch (for flat trajectory) to 11/32nds of an inch with .019-inch wall (for heavy
bow—80–100 pounds—durability). Coding of Easton shafts
is by a single, four-digit number. The first two numbers
designate the diameter in 1/64ths inches, while the second
shows the wall thickness in thousandths. For example, the
number 1618 means that the shaft is 16/64th (or ¼) of an
inch in diameter, while the wall thickness is .018 inch.

Unfortunately, aluminum arrows remain expensive; shafts
alone cost $20 to $30 a dozen. Manufacturers will straighten
not badly bent arrows for about 50 cents each. Best bet is for
the beginner in target archery to start with wooden shafts,
move to fiberglass when he stops losing arrows, graduate to
aluminum when he rarely misses the target.

Wooden arrows

In the early days of American archery, Norway pine was
tops for arrows until someone thought to try a little-known
and rare wood known as Port Orford cedar. Today Port
Orford cedar is recognized as the best of the woods. It got
its name from the Duke of Orford who in 1720 noticed odd
cedar trees growing along a 150-mile stretch of the coast of

Oregon and part of California. The only other place it is reported to grow is on Formosa.

Though lightweight, straight-grained and with fine spine properties, Port Orford cedar shafts have a tendency to break near the point, or to wear out and warp. These problems are decreased significantly, however, as a result of a process patented by Wm. E. Sweetland of Eugene, Oregon. In this, Port Orford cedar is compressed to about half its size. (Such shafts are sold under the trade names Forgewood or Battleshafts.) This process produces a much tougher arrow with greatly reduced warpage, and allows smaller-diameter shafts to be used with heavier bows. Compressed shafts are so strong, in fact, that they can be hammered through ¾-inch plywood. Compressed Port Orford cedar arrows, considered the best wooden shafts in the world, cost about $1.50 each.

Norway pine is second to cedar as an all-round wood. Many so-called "training" arrows are of birch, a wood that will take a lot of abuse, but is heavy and warps easily.

Wooden shafts are classified as *self* and *footed*. A self is made from a single piece; a footed arrow has a V-shaped length of tough wood—hickory, purple heart, beefwood—spliced into its point end. Withstands a higher degree of shock that way. In the case of a footed compressed wood shaft, the forward end is compressed to a higher degree than the rest of the shank.

Footed arrows cost somewhat more than self ones, and whether or not they are worth it is open to question. Some say the additional weight of 30 grains or so (there are 437.5 grains in an ounce) demands too high a trajectory. Light arrow shafts are highly prized in the tournament field for smooth, accurate shooting. In hunting, the picture changes; some seasoned bowhunters (but by no means all) feel that a heavier shaft gives better penetration.

Most wooden arrows are uniform in thickness from head to toe, are generally manufactured in sizes from 9/32nds to ⅜ of an inch in diameter, depending on bow weight—the heavier the thicker, as indicated in this chart:

Arrow Length:	16″	18″	22½″	24″	25″
Bow Weight: 15–27 lbs.	9/32″	9/32″	9/32″	9/32″	9/32″
28–35 lbs.				9/32″	9/32″
36–45 lbs.				5/16″	5/16″
46–60 lbs.					21/64″
60 lbs.					21/64″

Arrow Length:	26″	27″	28″	29″	30″
Bow Weight: 15–27 lbs.	9/32″	9/32″	5/16″	5/16″	5/16″
28–35 lbs.	5/16″	5/16″	5/16″	21/64″	21/64″
36–45 lbs.	5/16″	5/16″	21/64″	11/32″	11/32″
46–60 lbs.	21/64″	21/64″	11/32″	11/32″	11/32″
60 lbs.	11/32″	11/32″	11/32″	11/32″	11/32″

Some arrows taper gradually toward both ends. Such *barreled* arrows provide higher stiffness for given weights. Occasionally you run across a set of *crested* arrows, which are thicker in diameter under the fletching. Another type is the *bobtail*, which has the maximum diameter at the point, tapers gradually and uniformly back to the nock. Both are supposed to add stability but it's doubtful that they have any real effect. Conventional parallel-sided arrows cost about a third less than curved or tapered shafts.

More important than the shape is an arrow's spine, a term designating a shaft's relative bendability plus its springiness or recovery time. Spine controls the speed at which an arrow straightens out and stops undulating when it leaves the bow. An arrow too limber has a tendency to bend or buckle as it starts its flight. One that is too stiff tends to hit the side of the bow as it is released. Both extremes cause target misses.

Relative stiffness is determined by a spine tester, a gadget that supports an arrow near its ends while a 2-pound weight is applied to the center. The less the deflection, the stiffer (higher spined) the arrow.

Unfortunately, the spine tester doesn't tell the whole story. The *time* that a shaft takes to return to normal is also of the utmost importance. Further, there isn't any universally accepted code that the archer can make use of. Until arrow-making companies get together and decide on a common, relative set of figures (as the oil companies did with oil-weight numbers), the archer's best hope is to present bow weight, arrow length, and the kind and weight of point wanted to his supplier, and let him figure out the answer from the manufacturers' tables.

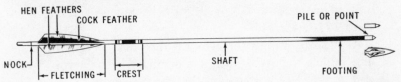

TERMINOLOGY OF ARROW PARTS

Courtesy, Bear Archery Co.

On the shaft, just down from the fletching, is a series of colored bands called the crest, a carry-over from medieval times when the colors duplicated family coats of arms. A crest today serves a threefold purpose. First, it still serves as a distinguishing mark; an archer can recognize his arrow immediately. Second, it adds a touch of beauty. And last, the flash of color may lead to fewer lost arrows.

It's a good idea for bowmen to personalize their crests. Though manufacturers offer a broad range, it's not uncommon for two archers to show up with identical crests, and unless there's something to distinguish them, scoring becomes a real problem. One solution is to paint over one of the crest bands. Another method is to buy crest decals, available from most large tackle shops. These can be used whole over the existing crest, or they can be cut apart. The wrap-on decals, usually in "Day-Glo" neon colors (for easy spotting), cost about a dollar a dozen.

So that lost arrows might be later returned by neighborly archers, some shooters print their names with India ink on the shaft below the crest. Others type their names along decal edges before applying, then give a squirt of plastic finish, protection from dampness.

Quality matched sets have the arrows numbered so each can be identified. If one arrow consistently shoots to the outside of a target, the bowman knows the fault is with the arrow, not himself, and can replace the arrow with another. A quickly discarded bad arrow in a tournament means a higher score. Also, a good archer gets to know the idiosyncrasies of each of his arrows—No. 5 flies a little low; No. 2 edges toward 10 o'clock, etc.

At the very top of the arrow is the nock, a cap with a slit into which the string fits. Unfortunately, the term "nock" also applies to the place on the string where the arrow fits, as well as to the ends of the bow where the string is held, plus, as a verb, to the act of fitting the arrow to the string. These are differentiated by saying "arrow nock," "bow nocks," "nocking point," and "to nock" or "nocking," respectively.

Not long ago the arrow nock was merely a slot sawed into the arrow end, sanded smooth, with perhaps a bit of thread wrapped around so the shaft wouldn't split. Old books spent pages explaining just how this slit should be made. No such trouble today. Replaceable plastic nocks (selling at less than a nickel each) are now nearly universal. The most popular kind has a molded index bump on one side in the same plane as the cock feather (the odd one), so that the arrow can properly be placed into position by feel. Nocks are brightly colored, easier to spot. Bright red or yellow nocks are best for spring and summer use, while blue or white ones stand out against fallen leaves in the autumn. Red is best for use in the snow.

To replace a nock, simply cut off the old one, sand or scrape away the old cement, glue on the new nock. The arrow will be ready for work in 20 minutes. (And next time you see a western movie, impress your friends by commenting on the Indians' plastic nocks.)

Just down from the nock—ordinarily about an inch or an inch and a quarter (this zone is called the butt)—is the fletching, an old English word which means feathers. (If your name is Fletcher, one of your ancestors was an arrow-feather sticker-onner.) Feathers correspond to the lands or "rifling" in a rifle barrel, serving to guide and stabilize the projectile's flight.

On target arrows, the three (occasionally up to eight) feathers are somewhere around ½ inch high, 2½ to 3 inches long; field or roving arrows have heavier, longer feathers—4 inches or so; hunting arrows range to 5½ inches or more.

Used to be you'd see nothing but gray goose feathers on arrows. Now turkey feathers—usually from toms—are most widely used. But here's another area where plastic may finally triumph. To an old archer, it looks rather silly to see flimsy bits of plastic stuck where feathers ought to go—until it rains, and the plastic stays fresh as the feather feathers droop. Maybe feathers will eventually go the way of sawed-in arrow nocks. Plastic vanes, particularly the larger sizes, usually need special arrow rests that attach to the bow to keep the fletching from smacking as it whisks by.

The trouble until recently was that plastic fletching couldn't be glued on tightly enough; now manufacturers seem to have licked the problem. (The American Indian, incidentally, didn't have this trouble. He didn't use glue. Instead, he bound eagle, hawk, buzzard or woodpecker feathers to his shaft with sinew, a practice which led to very unstable flight conditions—one reason the Indian was such a bad shot.)

On any given arrow, feathers are all from the same side of a bird. One, the so-called cock feather (usually of a different color) juts out at a right angle to the bow, with the other two equally spaced 120 degrees away. When four feathers are used, they're most often set at 75 and 105 degrees, but *can* be set at right angles. More than three feathers should not be used with hunting equipment; the extra fletching causes too much air resistance, and calls for such trimming that a high-speed hunting arrow will be unstable.

Fletching is attached either parallel with the shaft or on a spiral to give additional spin. (Some spin is imparted by the feathers' natural curvature.) The amateur is advised to use either parallel or slightly spiraled fletching in target arrows, mainly because nobody's proved the worth one way or the other, except that a smoother form is needed to get a helical fletched arrow off to a good start. It is, however, easier to see in the target. When using broad-point hunting arrows, some feather spiral apparently is necessary; otherwise a crosswind can cause planing, the tendency of a flathead to sail on the wind instead of through it. Spinning cuts down on the problem, though too much spin can cause noise, a serious thing for a hunter.

Shape of feathers is another controversial area. But though feathers have gone through a variety of evolutionary changes, the shape (within reason) seems to make little difference to an arrow's flight—so long as all are trimmed alike and have a total surface large enough to balance the other end.

Two kinds of flu-flus, used for flying targets: Bear's six-feathered cedar model and Saunders' Flu-fly, a plastic slip-on. Both kinds increase air resistance so that flights are shortened.

In addition to rubber-fletched fishing arrows, two other special-purpose missiles require special-purpose fletching. One is a flight arrow—designed for one thing only: distance. It uses plastic vanes. These give little resistance, little guidance. The other is the flu-flu (also spelled floo-floo and even frou-frou), an arrow with tightly spiraled or extra heavy feathers to slow it. Odd. It's for bird bowhunting. You can use your full draw, point at the sky, and not have to traipse into the next township to find your shaft. Flu-flus are quite accurate up to about 60 yards. Saunders Co. makes a plastic "flu-fly," for converting ordinary arrows to flu-flus. Looks like a badminton shuttlecock.

Now for the other end of the arrow—the point or more formally, pile (if there is no sharp hunting edge). Pick up an archery-equipment catalog; if you're unprepared you'll be astonished, and more than a little confused, at the array of points presented: half a dozen different target piles, a couple dozen hunting varieties (including everything from bull-frog to gar points), "shotgun" points, points that whistle, heads with no piles at all, rubber ones, and heads with spring-out bird snares.

Actually, with few exceptions (flight, for example), heads are divided into three general classifications: target, field and hunting. Target points are small, shaped in a "no skid" design—something like a cone set onto a tube; if the target is missed, they have a tendency to stick into the ground, not slither under the grass. Target points also are available in a not-so-good bullet design. If drawn to the correct position adjacent to the bow, these have a tendency to allow the arrow to point slightly to the right. Regular "parallel pile" target points have straight shoulders, and the problem just isn't.

Field points are heavier than those for conventional target practice. They're comparable in weight to hunting points, and are used as practice in the field. Some are flat-ended or have rubber points so you don't have to dig them out of trees. Others have points with threads; they can (in theory) be screwed out of stumps. A new kind of combination target and field point is Zwickey's "Judo." This device looks something like a conventional blunt-end point with four springs jutting out just back of the point. These 1) stop the point from penetrating too far into targets, and 2) jerk the

Zwickey's "Judo" field point has spring prongs that catch grass, snapping arrow upright. Arms also stop point from penetrating more than a fraction of an inch.

arrow bolt upright in the grass—easier to spot, and prevents "dig-in" and burrowing. The springs cause no detectable change in the flight pattern. Better not use them on game birds when you're using dogs, however; the metal extensions are likely to damage the animals' mouths.

Just because field points weigh the same as hunting points, however, is no reason to expect the two to fly alike. It just doesn't work that way. If you are practicing to hunt, the best idea is to get some cheap broadheads and shoot them into soft targets, or charge off a dozen points in advance. Before you start on the hunt, test your broadhead style under varying wind conditions to make sure you've selected a kind with minimum planing.

Hunting points come in broadhead, flathead, and bodkin styles, among others. Broadheads are flat, two- three- or four-bladed spear-shaped points. They're used for larger game—pig-size and up. According to rules of NFAA (National Field Archery Association) and the laws of most states, broadheads must be at least ⅞ of an inch wide with a cutting edge of at least ½ inch, which when hunting should be honed to a razor edge. The Zwickey broadhead sharpness test: Rest tip of edge on light string held horizontally. Holding arrow lightly at nock, slide cutting edge forward across string once. If edge is sharp enough, the string will sever.

Flatheads (blunts) have flat ends. They kill by shock, a very effective method for small game. If you're after squirrel, these points rarely leave your arrow sticking in a treetop.

Bodkins are stiletto-like, long, slender points with diamond-shaped cross sections. A good modern bodkin can sever a spinal cord, penetrate a skull, or cut through three or four inches of living bone. Dangerous.

Random sampling of point styles (left to right): cross-bladed razorhead (single-blade broadhead with crosswise auxiliary blade), three-bladed hunting head, field point, blunt roving point, and parallel-pile target point.

Points courtesy Bear Archery Co.

Some sets of hunting points on the market include a number of different heads that screw on the shaft, for easy changing in the field.

In a class by themselves are the fishing heads—somewhat similar to broadheads, but either barbed or equipped with safety-pin-like shanks that automatically spring open.

Points fasten to shafts in one of four ways: 1) *Slipover* points have holes the same diameter as the shaft. For target work, the rear edge often is beveled to make removal easier. 2) *Undercut* points have outside diameters the same size as the shaft; thus the shaft must be thinner in the point area in order to slip in. Theory here is that they're more easily pulled out of targets. The trouble is that this thinner wood makes breakage more common than with the slipover type, so these are not recommended for rough use. 3) *Taper-hole* points slip over 5-degree shaft tapers and are made to be interchangeable. Glued on with a special cement that softens with heat, these can be changed in the field with the help of a match. Taper-hole points are very strong, particularly recommended for rough field use. 4) *Insert* points slip inside aluminum or fiberglass shafting, are also interchangeable, and are strongest of all.

Chapter 5

WHAT ELSE DO YOU NEED?

EVERY so often you run across a bowman who disdainfully rejects the archer's two skin protection devices—leather guards for fingertips and forearms. He'll say that he feels the string better with a bare hand, adding that if an archer holds his arm correctly, the string won't slap it.

The bowman is right on both counts. But I, for one, refuse to shoot without something to protect my fingers and wrist. One reason: I've tried shooting without a wrist covering, and carried a goose-egg-size bump for three days to prove it. Another: I once knew a bowman who had shot so long without a fingertip protector that, like a bass player in a combo, he had developed thick calluses over his three shooting fingers. Then during a Sunday afternoon tournament he caught the string at the rough edge of the middle finger callus, and quick as a snit zipped the whole callus off. Messy.

Wrist guard

Theoretically, you need no protection for the bow arm at all; the string should whiz by without touching. But relax that arm too much, or shoot off a poor round (everyone does occasionally) and you're likely to shave off a layer of skin along the tender inside forearm. The arm guard or bracer has no detrimental effect on the shooting (a few archers use a style that *requires* the string to deflect off the guard),

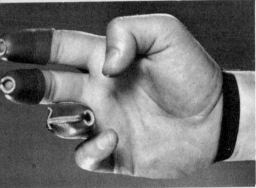

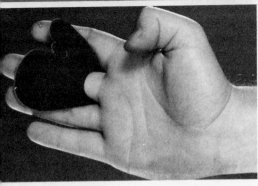

Wrist guard, shooting glove and finger tab.

and in the field it may even help by holding flapping jacket cuffs back out of the way.

Guards are secured to the arm by elastic, thongs, or straps. Elastic may wear out faster but because the hand can slip in and out quickly without lacing, more bowmen prefer it. Good guards are made of leather reinforced with spring-steel stays. Cheaper models often are stiff, and by the time they're worn in, they're worn out. The difference between top and bottom grade guards is only a couple of bucks.

Ventilated guards are more comfortable in the heat of summer. Be sure to get one long enough so that the string doesn't catch behind it. You can also buy a guard made of plastic, if you want to. You don't.

Some women (and an occasional man) have "double-jointed" elbows that bend backward a bit. Sometimes you see these unfortunates wearing bracers stretching from wrist to elbow. They shouldn't. They should learn to avoid this elbow lock by forcing the left shoulder down, and holding the forearm at a slight angle.

In an emergency, a folded handkerchief will substitute for a guard for a while, or you can secure a pencil to your arm with a pair of rubber bands.

Finger guards

As a bowstring is drawn back, pressure builds up, and as it is released, an immense amount of friction develops on your fingertips. Even a ten-pound bow will make your bowstring fingertips raw during a day's shooting, and a heavy hunting bow can quickly form blisters, can even draw blood.

For protecting those three vital fingertips, archers in the Western world have developed two general types of guards: tabs and gloves. They not only preserve the fingers, but will give the archer a smoother release. Fingertips are naturally rough, especially after shooting a few rounds bare-fingered, but for consistency, the string must slip away with a smooth motion. Tabs or gloves insure this jarless, stickless motion.

Which is better? Here, another controversy. Many top-grade target archers—Jim Bell, 1962 NFAA champ, for example—prefer the tab, essentially a mitten-shaped oval of leather that lies across the fingers. They claim that it provides for smoother release than the glove, that a shooter can better "feel" the string. Hunters, on the other hand, usually prefer shooting gloves; these are always ready when needed, require no adjustment before shooting, thus are "faster."

One disadvantage to a glove is that it always covers the fingertips, making it difficult to find the arrow in the quiver, roll the nock to the index mark, and feel that the nock snugs the string during the draw. A shooting tab slips out of the way into the palm, so during the first few steps the fingers are bare. And because the sides of the fingers are exposed, the nock and string can be felt during the draw. This last point may become a disadvantage when shooting heavy, short bows; the fingers may become squeezed together at full draw because of the sharp angle of the string.

A tab ordinarily consists of an oval piece of tough, slippery, shell-Cordovan leather—to resist string grooving—backed with a softer piece of leather or padded with felt or rubber. A hole for the middle finger (some models have more than one hole) or a leather thong keeps it in place.

Tabs cost less than a dollar each, but if you like, you can make a variety of them from soft leather portions of old shoes or ladies' leather handbags.

The modern archer's glove is an outgrowth of the thimble-like tips or cots, rarely seen today. The commonest consists of three finger ends held tightly by elastic strands leading to a wrist band. These cost somewhere around $2.50. Also available are full-sized gloves often reinforced with pads of shell horsehide, with thumb and little finger missing. Full gloves usually are too hot in summer, but for chilly fall hunting, can hardly be beat. Another refinement: washable gloves with replaceable, snap-off tips of vinyl plastic.

When buying a glove, try on a number of styles until you

find a perfect fit. Probably it will be stiff. To break in a new glove (or tab) give it a good dousing with saddle soap, then follow with leather oil or conditioner. Some people first soak it in water, then shoot with the glove until it dries.

For some reason, manufacturers have a tendency to produce fine gloves with one big fault: the leather tips are too long; they cover the finger joints. These can easily be fitted, though, with a sharp pair of manicure scissors. You can make your own from an ordinary glove. Just cut away the unused finger and thumb, add a couple of ventilation slits, and sew leather (from an old shoe) to the tips.

Many archers carry talcum powder in their tackle kits; a dusting on the shooting tab or glove fingers reduces friction, provides for a smoother release. Incidentally, it's a good idea to keep your nails cut short, especially the forefinger of the string hand.

Quivers

When one-time U. S. archery champion Wm. H. Palmer, Jr., entered the 1925 tournament, his quiver consisted of an open-end cardboard box held together by one of his wife's stockings and attached to his belt with a giant safety pin. You don't see much of that sort of thing anymore. So many kinds of quivers are available—from a 4-arrow pocket pouch to a 3-dozen back behemoth—in such broad price ranges that almost everyone can get just about what he needs.

In one of G. Howard Gillelan's excellent archer columns appearing in *Outdoor Life* magazine, he cites the following as his idea of the perfect quiver:

> . . . one that's practical for hunting in brush and blind and at the same time holds enough fodder for extended practice sessions . . . has plenty of capacity, yet [is] sufficiently light to avoid being a burden. It must not chafe the wearer or cause extra perspiration. . . . It must offer some rotation to its load but can't be so stiff that it creaks and groans with the move-

ments of the archer. It must be easy for the hunter to reach and placed so he can pull out a broadhead arrow softly, safely, and with a minimum of movement. It can't be a hindrance to a bowman at any time, whether he's sitting on a log, crouched high on the branch of a tree, or crawling on hands and knees through a rhododendron thicket.

Gillelan points out that this quiver hasn't yet been invented. But you probably can find one that *almost* meets the requirements. If not, you might try developing your own— many others have.

Most widely used is the shoulder or back quiver, whose basic design has changed little over the past 5,000 years. Essentially, it's a leather bag slung across the back with the mouth just under the right shoulder (for right-handed shooters), with the multicolored arrow feathers sticking upward.

Courtesy, Browning Arms Co.

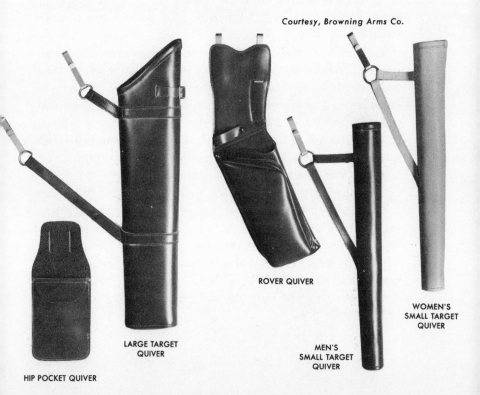

HIP POCKET QUIVER

LARGE TARGET QUIVER

ROVER QUIVER

MEN'S SMALL TARGET QUIVER

WOMEN'S SMALL TARGET QUIVER

Most quality store-bought shoulder quivers have one or more zippered pockets for carrying extra string, a knife, pliers (for removing broadheads from trees), rope, sharpening stone, a plastic fold-up raincoat, and maybe lunch. It may also have a window for a hunting license. Many quivers are divided into two sections—one for hunting points, the other for field heads. Most have sponge rubber in the bottom to protect sharp points, an essential. This type quiver runs from about $2 for an imitation-leather (cardboard or plastic) model to $30 for a flashy, calfskin-covered golf bag with the hair left on.

The best ones have an extra strap that runs under the bowhunter's armpit. Without this, the quiver has a tendency to slide down the back, and when the bowman reaches over for a quick shot, he grabs nothing. However, when crawling through brush or barbed-wire fencing, the archer must unsnap this extra strap to allow the quiver to slide down and around under the arm; otherwise he'd have to go through backwards.

This kind of quiver has three big disadvantages to the hunter: For one thing, the arrows tend to rattle as the bowman attempts to sneak through the bush—and when you consider that nearly everything has better hearing than you, the problem looms large. Secondly, there usually is nothing to keep the arrows in this traveling trunk—dramatically apparent when the hunter stoops over to get under a low branch. And finally, the arrows can't be sneaked out. Come upon a deer, freeze, and the animal may be alerted but not take off; reach your hand above your head to grasp an arrow, pull it high enough to get out of the quiver, then fit it, and long-gone will be the venison.

To get around the problem, at least one manufacturer puts out a shoulder quiver with a large window near the bottom. With this one you can slip the arrows out point first, behind your back.

An even sneakier type is the hip or belt quiver. This often attaches to the waist with two straps, long enough so that the bag can be swiveled from feather-front position (for easy grabbing) to fletch-rear, for traveling through brush. These also are adequate for target shooters, as hip quivers are easily unsnapped and left standing on the ground while the archer removes his arrows from the target. One disadvantage to this type is that many archers tire of the disconcerting thwack of the quiver against their legs.

Also made for hunting—but more useful on the field range —is the relatively rare vest quiver, or rather, an archer's vest with a quiver built in. These are nicely made with fine, large pockets handy for carrying extra tackle, field glasses, etc., but the quiver part is sewn on, is nonadjustable, and can really hang you up in a bramble patch.

Then there's the arm quiver, a gadget that straps to the left arm and carries about four arrows pretty much out of the way—good for those bowhunters accurate enough not to need extras.

With somewhat more capacity is the pocket quiver, designed to be worn on the rump. Some slip into the pocket; others snap over the belt. Many have separate doodad pouches. Old target bowmen simply use their back pocket, usually after first lining it with a flap of leather, inserted fold down.

Most interesting modern arrow holders fit right on the bow. They don't hold many arrows—two to five—but when traveling through rough territory the hunter has only one implement tangling in the brush to worry about. Best thing about bow quivers is that the arrows always are ready to be whipped into place. And by the time one missile strikes the target, another can already be nocked. There's a wide variety to choose from, everything from a one-piece, plastic model selling for about a dollar to a deluxe, permanently installed screw-on device costing $10 or more. Screw-on models are not good; the screws will likely weaken your bow, leading to splits or sudden breakage. A better idea is tape—may seem sloppy, but it works fine.

If you're the kind of hunter who goes for deer and rabbits simultaneously, and want a few practice arrows along for an occasional stump shot, perhaps two quivers is the best idea —one bow or arm quiver, one pocket or back quiver.

For the target shooter, a ground quiver is a handy device. This consists of a piece of $\frac{3}{16}$-inch-diameter steel, brass or aluminum wire, sharpened on one end, bent into a 4-inch loop on the other. Stick it in the ground and drop your arrows through the loop, points down. Price about $1.50 (with a top-side bow holder, $3); or, made from a wire coat hanger (if you're not anxious about sturdiness), free.

Chapter 6

TARGETS

A TARGET can be anything an arrow will penetrate —stumps, anthills, clapboard walls, tin cans—but few materials can take bombardment without either breaking up or ruining arrows. Because arrows are the most delicate equipment in the tackle box, and because they represent the largest single expense item on your archery bill, it pays the bowman to practice on legitimate targets only.

The regulation target archery face is 4 feet in diameter, usually of oilcloth. The center golden (usually yellow) bull's-eye is 9.6 inches across. Surrounding it are concentric rings of red (usually sun-faded to a sickly orange), 19.2 inches in diameter; blue, 28.8 inches across; black, diameter of 38.4 inches; and white, which fills out the rest of the 48 inches. Note that each ring is 4.8 inches wide, which means that the total of both sides of each ring is 9.6, the diameter of the bull's-eye. (The gold may have a 3-inch black spot in the center—called a "pimple" among the knowing—for those who can really zero in.)

Standard height for the target is 48 inches above the ground at the center. (These target sizes and values apply only to *target* archery; for field target specs, see Chapter 13.) A 4-foot target face and backing is devilishly awkward to lug around if you don't have an easel on wheels. The next smallest conventional size is a yard across, and a 2-foot model also is available. For tyro archers, it's best to get the largest target practical, keeping in mind the work required to move it. At first, the novice will be missing the whole thing a good part of the time, and he'll quickly tire of shagging arrows snaked under the grass. Also, to the beginner (in fact, to all archers), that "thwunk" as the arrow strikes is a pleasant sound, and the larger the target the more frequent the thwunks.

Value of the target bands are:

White	1
Black	3
Blue	5
Red	7
Gold	9

Beginning archers often wonder why a simple 1, 2, 3, 4, 5 sequence isn't used. For this, two answers. First, the area of the entire target face is about 25 times that of the gold. Therefore, if the white were given a value of 1 point, the gold should be worth 25 points, the others: red, 6.250; blue, 2.777; and black, 1.563. At long range this would work out pretty well. At short range, however, the *excellent* archer would be given an unfair advantage over a *good* archer; his strikes, mainly in the inner rings, would add up too quickly, making the man who never misses the target, but who who is more often than not in the outer rings, look terrible when scores are posted. Besides, who wants to add up all those decimals? So—we arbitrarily give the rings 9, 7, 5, 3, 1 values, and though the superior archer is recognized, he doesn't overwhelm the opposition.

Second, there's an interesting mathematical ratio to the rings. They are all equal in cross section (the diameter of the outer edges, minus the inner), and if the center disc represents one unit, the red ring counts for three units (the diameter is three times that of the gold), the blue has a value of five (five times the diameter of the gold), etc. Invert the whole thing, and you have the gold counting for nine, the red, seven, and so on to white, which counts one. O.K.?

At least the system has stood the test of time. Although changes in value have been attempted, it looks like the system will be ever with us. Incidentally, many sports shops carry handy little score keepers that automatically tally when you press a button the proper number of times. If you like gadgets, this is a good one.

A suggestion here: Record your scores even when you first start shooting. The advantage is psychological: You'll be amazed at how quickly you progress. Your archery dealer has score cards on which you can keep your progress history.

In tournament archery, arrows ordinarily are shot in groups of six, and each batch is called an *end*. A complete game, called a *round*, is made up of a certain number of ends. Noncompetitive rounds usually stop when one of the shooters gets tired, it begins to rain, or a local cow devours the straw target. (Standard tournament competition rounds are listed in Chapter 14.)

Custom has it that in each end, higher-value arrows are noted first. Withdraw your best arrow and write down the value; pull out the next best and record it in the next column, etc. (A perfect end counts 54—6 times 9.) If you shoot from more than one distance, custom again has it that you stand at the longest distance first. Probably because it's nicer to end the day with the best scores.

Front to rear, a typical target consists of three layers: a fabric or paper *face*, a tightly woven grass *matt* of from two to some seven inches thick—circular and a little larger than the face—and a *butt*, a word originally meaning a "hill of sod." The words "matt" and "butt" are now often used interchangeably, and incorrectly. The matt section often is skipped in field-type targets.

Regulation matts are 50 inches in diameter and from 4 to 6 inches thick; they (and the target) lean away from the archer at an angle of from 12 to 18 degrees.

Various tightly wound grasses and marsh hays are used in the majority of matts. Rye straw and Johnson grasses are good, as is a special grass variety called Spartana Indian cord. Wheat has short, weak stalks, with too short a target lifetime to be of much use.

Some matts have extra-tough centers, with the arrow entering parallel to the fibers, spreading them with little damage. When the arrow is withdrawn the wound is self-healing. You might check for this feature before you lay down your money. Two other premiums you might ask about: chemical treatment to discourage rodents and rot, and hand stitching which allows the cords to be tightened when they become loose.

Occasionally, cut-rate matts are available. Their mortality rate more often than not reflects the price. Before buying one of these, try to stick a pencil into it; if you easily can, arrows will sail through before long.

Quality 2-foot matts run somewhere around $10; 3-foot models about $15, and regulation size about $25. A protective burlap covering adds about $2. Sears Roebuck sells a 2-foot wood fiber and cardboard matt-target combination for about $3. Alone, it won't last long, but used as facing for one of the more expensive matts, it gives excellent results.

For light bows—under 40 pounds—your dealer might stock various "core" matts, highly compressed cardboard discs sandwiching layers of sisal (a hemp). These wear more quickly than straw targets, but for the price—less than $10 for a 3-foot target—they may be worth trying.

A relatively recent addition to target technology is the "arrowstop." The front of this unit is made of loose, end-grain marsh grass. The arrow penetrates parallel to the fibers, separating instead of cutting them. Slowed to about half speed, the arrow then hits free-hanging composition plates inside the box, which "give" three or four inches, with the arrow actually pushed back slightly through the front as the inside sections return to their original position. This type is expensive—about $60 for a 28-inch target mounted in a 30-inch-square box. But those who have used it say it outlasts any other kind.

Round target matts *can* be made at home, but it's a hard, dirty job. If you want to attempt it, here is a method described by Dr. Robert P. Elmer, one-time U. S. Champion, in his oft-quoted *Archery:* "Squeeze as much straw as you can into a four-inch diameter and bind it with strong tarred cord. . . . When the length is about 2½ feet, double it over on itself and sew it firmly together with a whip stitch, using the tarred cord and a large curved sacking needle eight inches long or a mattress needle. By feeding more straw into the rope, always keeping it four inches thick, and sewing round and round, you finally, with much sweat of the brow, find that the diameter has reached four feet." The somewhat elongated shape can be made round by stuffing in extra straw where needed.

An effective small-matt enlarger can be made from an old auto or truck tire. With an economical matt slipped into the tire, the arrow-stopping area is enlarged almost four times. When an arrow hits the tire, it bounces back instead of slithering under the grass in the rear. Best method is to cut the tire at the top (you'll need a hack saw to get through the bead) and bore a hole in the bottom for water drainage. Bore a couple more holes—one on either side of the cut—and thread a rope through to pull the split together. At four points around the tire loosely loop four ropes. Open the tire a little, slip in the matt, pull the cut tight, and snug things up with the four edge ropes.

Common target stands are either of metal rods or wood. Metal ordinarily is a poor idea; each glancing blow likely means a pointless arrow. If you already have a metal-legged stand, cover the rods with split garden hose, or wrap them closely with two layers of clothesline.

One of the best stands is the cheapest, and easiest to make. It consists of three 1-by-3-inch pine boards, 6 feet long. A half-inch hole is bored near one end of each. With a single loose-fitting bolt through these holes, the three boards make a tripod. The target is hung from the apex, resting against two of the legs. To steady the arrangement so wind doesn't blow it over, a rope is tied at the top, then staked to the ground under the tripod's center. A cut-apart bicycle tire can be nailed flat against the two front legs to guard against arrows sticking in the wood. If you use no rubber guard, don't bevel the wood in front; leave it square. It's better to remove arrow heads with pliers than to have them snap from the shaft as they glance off.

A pair of pliers, by the way, is a good tool to keep permanently in your tackle box. When an arrow is stuck and the shaft can't easily be turned by hand, a twist with the pliers *on the point* should loosen it easily. When the point penetrates part of the target and digs into the underlying wood, try the usual method of removal (a slight twist with the right hand while pressing the target with the left), and if that doesn't work, try *pushing*, while turning and wiggling. Another course of action: Pull on the arrow while bashing the target with your fist or a rock. Last recourse: Take the target apart or twist the shaft with pliers. You'll lose the point, but may save the arrow.

If a point comes off inside the matt, shove the arrow into the wound again and push it all the way through.

Sometimes the head disappears into a target leg or nearby tree. You'll have to cut the wood away with a knife or small chisel in this case. (A sheathed chisel is another good tool to carry with you.) Same thing when a broadhead sinks itself into a tree—a twist will simply shear off the blade.

Temporary, inexpensive target matts can be made from corrugated cardboard. Purchased in rolls many feet long in widths somewhere around 15 inches, the cardboard should be rerolled very tightly. A close-fitting oilcloth cover, onto which the face is affixed, finishes the job.

Another temporary matt can be made by gluing several

thicknesses of corrugated cardboard together. Cut up a number of grocery-store boxes and piece the sections to form a matt of, say, four inches thick. When the center becomes worn, you can, with a little work, rip out the broken section and stick in a new one.

Nested corrugated boxes, with spaces between filled with sand (no pebbles) and excelsior also have been used with more or less success. Unless stuffed tightly, however, high-powered bows will soon shoot arrows all the way through.

The most satisfactory stationary target butts or backstraps are bales of wild hay. They're cheap and easy to get. When you buy hay bales, make sure they are tightly packed and compressed with wire, not rope. Burlap wrapped around them will prevent grass from littering the range. Second choice seems to be the more expensive excelsior.

A stand for a three-bale butt can be made from two old tires, a pair of 2-by-2-inch poles, some strong wire, and heavy tarpaper or oilcloth. The tires raise the hay off the ground and stop the arrows, unharmed, from sliding underneath.

Place the two tires side by side on the ground and lay a bale atop them, bands running across the top and bottom. With a sledge, pound the poles (metal pipes can be used if covered with a split garden hose) into the ground between the back of the bale and the inside of the tires. Run the wire through the bale bands and affix them to the poles. Wire the upper two bales in place, horizontally, in the same way. The tarpaper or oilcloth is for weather protection. Attach it with giant-size staples made from wire coat hangers. The butt should last a couple of years with moderately heavy use.

Perhaps the simplest butt-holder consists of a base to keep the bales off the ground and a prop to hold them upright. Here is a plan for making a five-bale butt from scrapwood: Nail boards across 2 two-by-fours to make a platform large enough to hold a horizontal bale (about 2 feet by 3½ feet).

Typical field course target, this one on the range of Lincoln Park Archers, near Towaco, N. J.

Sink the back of the platform in the ground (or prop up the front) so that it tilts, giving a slant to the target. Pile dirt in front to prevent arrows from skittering into the base. Place one bale flat on the platform at right angles to the line of flight, stand up another bale in the center of the first one, and flank it by two others. Top these with the fifth bale, placed like the first. You now have a horizontal bale supporting three vertical ones, capped by another horizontal bale.

Wrap the whole thing with two circles of fairly heavy galvanized wire. Slip a stout stick between the two wires, and wind one wire around the other to make the structure rigid. Use another stick to do the same thing on the other side. To prop the thing steady, wedge a board in the back at an angle between the ground and the center of the topmost bale. Stuff extra straw into the open places between bales. Keep out weather with an old tarp or piece of linoleum; or staple oilcloth or tarpaper with large staples made from coat hangers or with commercial bale staples.

Though butts of wild hay are best for field courses, a beginning club usually cannot afford enough bales for the full round. Satisfactory substitutes, in areas where practical, are butts of sod or clay. Usually, however, rocks present too great a threat. The National Field Archery Association suggests stopgap butts of large burlap bags stuffed with corrugated cardboard pieces and held apart by sawdust or tightly crammed excelsior. For a 24-inch target, seams are removed from two sacks, and the two burlap pieces combined with heavy twine and a sack needle to make a twice-as-big bag.

Tie the burlap butts between trees. They won't last long, but should get you through the first season, after which, hopefully, enough new members will join to warrant permanent straw butts.

In deciding where to place your vacant-lot targets, safety is the prime consideration. Though you may be a good shot, sooner or later you'll let a novice take a crack at it, and there's no telling where the arrows will fly. Make sure that there is enough open space to the sides and behind the tar-

Lacking butts of hay, excelsior, or other such material, a temporary substitute can be made from a double layer of newspaper bundles. Offset them so arrows won't sail through cracks.

get so that you will see anyone wandering into the area. Or, if this is impossible, keep-out ropes can be strung around the perimeter.

You can more easily control side-to-side aiming than your elevation angle, so it's better to give more latitude to range length than width. An archer will rarely miss the target by more than a foot or two to the sides, but a 30-foot overshot —particularly from a top-target glancing blow—is not uncommon even among better archers. (For target layout of field ranges, see Chapter 13.)

An ideal target location would be in front of a rockless sand dune. Lacking this, some other kind of backstop is a good idea—worth it in saved tempers, if nothing else. One kind is simply old rugs hanging on a rope strung ten feet or so in back of the target. Another backup is burlap *hurdles*, two or three rows of foot-high curtains hanging loose at the bottom, placed about ten feet apart. Or dig a series of small trenches in back of the target, at right angles to the line of flight; arrows, with a tendency to stick upright, will be easier to spot.

For basement or garage practice, Saunders Archery Target Company recommends the use of 2-inch-thick strawboard or insulation board. (See opposite page.)

A somewhat easier design involves the use of ¾-inch sheets of soft building board, usually available in 10-foot lengths, in various widths. No supporting structure is needed. To construct a backup, take two lengths and place one on top of the other, flat on the ground. Slide one to the side about four inches. Bore two holes through both at the top and tie loosely with clothesline. Bore another hole through both at the bottom. Set the structure upright in sort of a tepee arrangement—the tops together, the bottoms maybe two feet apart—then thread a rope through the bottom holes to keep the two boards from sliding too far apart.

Do the same with two other sheets (or more) and overlap each set the four inches. (You can run it down the whole

MATERIALS LIST

3—2x4—7' 7"

4—2x4—8' 3⅝"

4—2x4—3' 7⅞"

2—2x4—3' 10"

3—2x4—8'

3—2x4—3' 7"

1—2x4—7' 6¾"

10—2x4—0' 8"

2—2x4—0' 11"

3—2x4—1' 6"

2—4x8 Strawboard or insulation Board—2" thick

4—Commercial target brackets

BOLTS

6—⅜"x8" Sq. Head Bolts with wing nuts

15—¼x6" Carriage

16—¼x2" Carriage

90—¼x4" Carriage

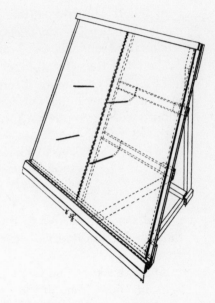

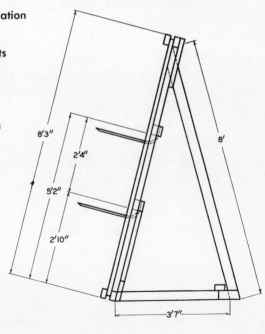

wall length.) Arrows often will penetrate the first board easily, but because the second is at an angle, will tend to wedge between. The day's shooting over, the boards can be pushed together for storage.

Local fire companies often object if a clubhouse uses a wallful of straw butts. Often the authorities can be placated if butts are fireproofed. A formula recommended by NFAA:

9 ounces sodium borate (Borax)
4 ounces boric acid
1 gallon water

Add some green dye to this solution and spray the butts thoroughly; the dye will help you to see that the straw is covered.

So far as I know, no target suitable for broadheads has yet been invented—though the various foam plastics now being tried seem promising. One field range uses upholsterer's padding backed by one-inch hardwood boards and held in place by a canvas cover. Broadheads penetrate the wood only a little and for the most part are fairly easy to extract. So claim the bowmen. But many heads are broken, and the targets have short life lines. Actually, an archer who knows his bow and who knows how to shoot arrows of the same weight as broadheads should be able quickly to shift over on the hunt.

More difficult is shooting at flying objects—and no article or book can tell you how to go about it. Best way to learn is to use sailing targets. Fortunately, this isn't as difficult as it might seem, with expendable targets and retrievable flu-flu arrows—those with feathers so fluffy that they cause the arrow to drop quickly.

Aerial shooters use such targets as pie plates, wooden tops of bushel baskets, plastic detergent bottles, old phonograph records, or squares of thin plywood or composition board. Saunders Co. makes a flying target called a "bowbird," a

A "bowbird" flying target is assembled . . .

. . . and while one archer throws it into the air, the other picks it off nicely.

heavy cardboard disk 15 inches in diameter with an "X"-shaped projection sticking up in the middle. A hollow airspace on the underside makes possible sailing the target slowly enough that a lone bowman has time to throw the thing, then shoot it down.

Difficult as shooting a flying object is, a bowhunter at

least has one very great advantage over a gunner: He can see the path of his arrow. Technique is similar to that of shotgunning. The archer moves his fully drawn arrow across the target's flight path, releases when he gets the correct distance ahead (no formula here), and continues to move forward, in the follow-through.

How many hits can you expect? G. Howard Gillelan, archery columnist for *Outdoor Life* magazine, has established a 1-in-12 ratio—one pheasant for every 12 shots—as par.

When you have both space and the energy required to make them, nonflying targets can add much, particularly if you make a club project of their construction. One rather unsatisfactory device is a target face attached to a bicycle tire, shot as it rolls down a hill. Arrows pass through, but you can tell where you hit by the hole. A batch of paper or cloth circles and Scotch tape are needed to patch the holes after every few rolls.

A better target is a pendulum, if you can find a tree with a stout branch set before a backstop hill. Mount a target on a two-by-four of suitable length, and attach this somehow (by ropes, a large bolt, a healthy-size hinge) to the branch so that it swings back and forth without twisting. Once the target gets swinging, it's possible to get in a fair number of shots before it stops. If possible, cover exposed wood with hacked-up tires.

A moving target using an inclined, number 9 wire or small-diameter cable can be made with a little imagination. Two trees 80 to 100 feet apart on a hillside is a good arrangement, or if you haven't hills on your range, tie one end of the wire high in one tree, near the ground on the other. To pull the target back up after a slide, you'll either have to climb a ladder or attach a line to the return rope so that it can be pulled from the ground. Or better, pick up an inexpensive battery-operated motor from a "government surplus" supply house to do the work for you. (The four national mechanics/

handicraft magazines carry ads for these.) Draw the wire tight with turnbuckles at both ends. The return rope should be just long enough so the target can't quite reach the end of the slide, and should be attached to the upmost point with a heavy spring or two to stop the target slowly.

The newest and most exciting thing to hit the target arena —particularly for club use—is the self-operated target return, an archery development comparable to the advent of bowling's automatic pinsetters. Designs and prices vary, but a typical unit might be represented by the Arrowmatic Target Return, by Trueflight. This system costs about $700 per target, and it consists essentially of a cart which runs on tracks,

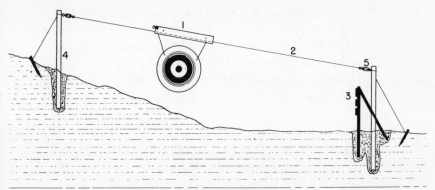

SLIDING TARGET DIAGRAM

Here is a sliding target arrangement worked out by Saunders Co. The roller frame (1), detailed at right, is of two 1 x 6 x 30-inch pieces of softwood; rollers are V-belt pulleys held away from frame with heavy washers. Length of #9 wire (2) is stretched tight by turnbuckles (5) attached to posts (4). Better idea than the target stopper (3) is a rope run between roller frame and upper post, cushioned with a heavy spring.

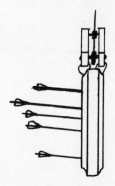

and a console to control it. The cart will carry 400 pounds of backstop (about five straw bales), takes up little more room than the bales alone, and is portable—can even be set up outside, if the ground is level.

You shoot your arrows, and instead of walking to the target, you punch a button and it comes to you. Travels about 3 mph, walking speed. Another button sends it back to whatever distance you want (to 60 feet or more), and it stops at the point within an inch. If an arrow drops in front, the target even has sense enough to brush it out of the way, instead of lumbering over it. (You have to pull the arrows out yourself.)

If none of the arrangements mentioned in this chapter work for you—if you still can't strike the target—last resort might be a system explored in a French short movie called *The Fat and the Lean*. An archer was shown shooting at a target held by his assistant. Whenever the arrow was loosed, the lackey would run to where it was headed, while the archer stood there looking very proud because his score was so high.

Chapter 7

STRINGS AND STRINGING

FOR the beginning archer, one of the toughest tricks is bracing (stringing) his bow. It is also one of the most dangerous. People have lost teeth, broken noses, and been knocked cold when trying to fit a string to a bow, and more good bows have been lost because of strings than anything else.

What then is this formidable component, the string?

First strings probably were of rawhide, then later of gut. Silk was an early favorite (because of its scarcity rather than its value), as was dried seaweed and an Irish flax spun under water. Metal strings also have been tried, but though they gave a pleasant twang when the arrow was released, the bowman never quite knew in which direction his missile would travel.

Old archery books spend thousands of words describing favorite methods of spinning, weaving and determining just which strength string is needed for what bow. Fortunately, the modern bowman needn't concern himself with the technical details unless he makes his own strings, for today's strings not only are good, but cheap.

Modern shops deal almost exclusively in three materials: Italian hemp (cheap, but short-lived—for bows under about 30 pounds), Irish linen (until relatively recently, *the* bowstring material), and DuPont's Dacron polyester fiber or other synthetic material (strong, durable, consistent). Popular, heat-stretched Dacron costs about three times that of other materials, but is well worth the extra—in lasting qualities, bow-break safeguards, and placid tempers. A few bowhunters prefer Flemish (or Laid) strings, claiming increased reliability, but they are in the minority. The fact is, most experts say that Dacron is so much better than anything else around that it is the only thing worth considering.

When buying strings today, the archer need specify only two things in addition to material: bow weight and string length—and even the store clerk can't make a mistake; the two figures are printed on the string box.

Bow weight you have; it's most likely stamped on the bow. String length you may have to figure, although most top companies now also print this on their bows. The best method is to measure your old string before you need a new one—assuming the old one is the correct size. Distance is measured between the inside edges of the end loops, with the string fully stretched and off the bow. Because it's a little tough to stretch an unstrung string tight, measure it from loop serving (the wound thread) to loop serving while strung, unbrace the bow, then measure the outstretched loops and add your figures.

But maybe your present string isn't right. Check it by noting the fistmele, the distance between the braced string and the bow belly. The "fistmele" originally was the distance from an average archer's thumb tip to the base of his clinched fist, a little more than six inches. This is still the standard (but not invariable) distance for flat-bow fistmeles. But working recurves are usually higher—to eight inches or more. The shorter the string, of course, the higher the fistmele.

When your bow is properly strung, check the fistmele with your fist, and note where the string comes on your thumb. This quick-check method will later be handy in the field, and is the method universally used by archers. If the correct-

Courtesy, West Coast Engineering

Typical indoor range is 24-target Downey Archery Lanes in Downey, Calif. Each console controls a target; a push of a button brings target forward. Another button rolls it back to any of six distances between 20 feet and 30 yards.

length string is too far from the bow for your thumb to reach when your fist is clenched, spread your hand and find some other measurement—perhaps the distance between your thumb tip and the first joint of your outstretched little finger, or that between your wrist and fingertips. Those whose arrows are all crested alike can use a pre-measured distance between the end of the nock and a particular crest band. (A few companies measure bracing height across the arrow shelf from the back of the bow to the nocking point.)

When the original string is lost and the fistmele is not stamped on the bow, you're in trouble. There is no set rule for determining the right length. For flat bows, you can get pretty close by measuring the length of the bow along the back (the convex side) from nock to nock, then subtracting about 3¼ inches. Recurve and other style bows are more difficult because they're measured as though they were flattened, and different bow materials work at varying degrees of tautness. If you have a recurve, try measuring with a flexible steel rule (nock-to-nock distance) and take off 3 inches. Or measure between the nocks on an unstrung bow; this distance equals string length exactly on many modern recurves. When you determine the approximate string length, brace the bow, shoot off a few rounds, and adjust the string just tight enough that it doesn't snap your hand.

Most strings are purchased with built-in loops. (When they're permanent, they're called *eyes*.) Some, however, have an eye in only one end; the bowman puts in the other (and here, the loop is called a *noose*) by tying a timber hitch —so named because lumberjacks used this kind to fasten hauling ropes to logs. It's a handy knot and easy to tie. When you find the correct length, you thereafter can buy strings with eyes at both ends.

Wrapped around the bowstring at the center and both ends is *serving* of nylon or other tough material. In commercial strings, the length of the center serving varies from about three to seven inches or so. The purpose of this is twofold: The enlarged string doesn't cut into the tab or glove fingers, and the serving protects the string from wear.

If you do your own serving, or if the original serving has become worn and needs replacement, you can use any number of materials: number 8 linen thread, heavy carpet thread, light gut, strands from a broken bowstring. Whatever you use, give it a good coating of beeswax (available from your dealer) before starting. Work should be done on a strung bow.

Start two inches or so from the center and lay out a half inch of thread along the string, free end toward the center. Wrap over it with the line snugly (but not too tight) until you come approximately to the same distance on the other side of the center. To make sure the thread doesn't unwind, wrap the last few turns loosely, then stick the free end under them and jiggle the loops closed, working from the tightly wrapped portion. Close the last loop by pulling on the thread end. Loop the end around the served string once more and knot it. Slice off the loose end with a razor blade. (But don't zip through the string; this, too, has happened.)

If you have an extra dollar or two, you might want to pick up a serving tool, a glorified spool holder. It helps. Coat the served portion of the string with Duco or similar cement for a smooth release.

The spot where the arrow and the serving meet is called the *nocking point*. Usually it's a hump in the string against which the arrow rests, a positive guide to assure the archer that he is placing his arrow on the same string spot each time. If you're looking for uniformity in shooting (and who isn't?) a nocking point is a must. To find the right point for nocking, fold a piece of paper over the string so that the paper's top side is lined up with the point at which the drawn arrow leans against the bow. Since most bows give best results if the drawn arrow points slightly downward, locate the nocking point about ⅛ of an inch above the place where the top of the paper falls on the string.

The easiest thing is to buy ready-made nocking points. One simple, effective kind consists merely of a pair of 2-inch plastic tubes, just large enough to slip over standard serving. Each tube has a slit along its length through which the string slips, one tube being placed toward the top of the bowstring, the other toward the bottom. Then the two are slid over the serving toward each other, stopping with a notch between slightly smaller than an arrow nock. The tubes are cemented in place. The too-small opening wedges the arrow nock just tight enough to hold it in place during the draw, but not so tight as to impede its release.

Most bowmen still prefer to wind their own nocking points. For this they usually use dental floss or ordinary sewing machine thread. This is wrapped around the nocking place until the arrow nock snugs in, then the winding operation moves up a bit and the hump is made. Some archers add another hump below the nocking place—holds the arrow from slipping up *or* down. In either case, humps are sealed in place with a few dabs of model airplane-type glue. Be sure you place the nocking point on your next string in the identical position.

If you find that your strings tend to wear at the loops, reinforce them with serving. The timber-hitched noose of a single-eyed string should always be reinforced or it will quickly wear where the knot is tied. (Before stringing, incidentally, make sure your bow nocks are smooth and free from splinters; if not, you'll need a new string before long.)

If all else holds, strings finally will part at the nocking point due to the friction of the strands rubbing together under the serving—and there's nothing to be done to prevent it. (Too-tight serving may aggravate the wear, however.) Strings should have a reserve of strength, so if one or two strands part, there's no need to get worried—just alerted.

When the string begins to look fuzzy and somewhat moth-eaten, cut off the loose ends to prevent further raveling, then give it a coating of bowstring wax—something called a "special compound" by manufacturers, but often as not merely a cake of beeswax. Rub it in briskly with a hunk of leather so that friction will melt it. Don't wax the center

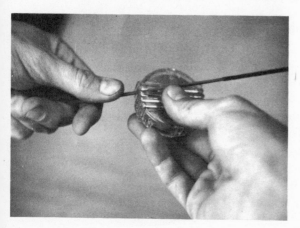

Beeswax keeps bowstring limber and water resistant. Plastic holder shown has slits through which string is drawn to pick up wax coating.

serving, or you'll find your shooting tab or glove sticking to it. When a few more strands begin to look bedraggled, better replace the string, for should it finally give way when the bow is fully drawn, the arms can very well spring forward with so much vigor they crack.

Eventually you'll notice that your arrows are beginning to land a little low on the target. This possibly indicates you're getting tired and aren't hauling back far enough. But it also might mean that your bowstring has lengthened. One old archer lived with his favorite bow so long that he could detect the drop in pitch when his bowstring needed tightening. When your arrows begin to drop, check the fistmele, and if it is less than desired, you can take up a little length by twisting the string, so long as the serving doesn't kink or loosen. Turn only in the direction of the original twist; the opposite way will weaken the string. Bowstring lengthening can be traced to age, temperature, humidity and, to a lesser extent, length of the shooting session.

It's a good idea to break in new strings with an hour's worth of shooting before adding them to your tackle box. Watch that your spare string doesn't unwind when you put it away. A good storage container, by the way, is a plastic toothbrush tube.

Now to brace the bow. Somewhere I once saw instructions on how to string a bow on horseback, while crossing a stream, while lying down, and while wounded. Because it's doubtful that many will find the instructions useful, we'll consider only the two most widely used methods—the standard, for bracing flat bows and low-weight recurves, and the step-through, for heavier recurves.

"When a beginner comes into my shop," says L. E. Stemmler, Manorville, N. Y., manufacturer of archery equipment, "one of my first questions is if he knows how to string a bow. . . . The eager novice either tries to climb the bow like a monkey . . . or grabs it by the top and attempts to drive it into the floor. . . . Others contort themselves into horrible shapes, wrap one leg around the bottom limb and yank the top limb east by west.

"These ways will spring the lower limb all out of shape," Stemmler continues, "and the result is usually a bow that will no longer bend evenly. . . . The proper method is an easy, simple, graceful maneuver."

For Mr. Stemmler, yes. But not for most of the rest of us, if we're talking about an 80-pound recurve. I have yet to see anyone brace one of these without at least a grimace. By any method. Nevertheless, the "standard" method is the safest and, if you can learn to do it in an "easy, simple, graceful maneuver" more power to you.

The following, by the numbers, is the standard method for a north paw. To some archers, it will seem backwards. For me, it works. If you don't feel comfortable, try reversing "left" and "right." If you're brand-new to the game, that won't feel right either. Nothing will. (Try it with a very light bow first, if one is available. Switch to the heavier one when you have developed the knack.)

1. Most bowstrings have a little eye and a big eye. Place the big eye over the top end of the bow and slide it down over and past the nock. It should slip to somewhere around five inches from the top before it snugs to a stop. The bottom end of the string now should be dangling somewhere around the bow end. Slip it over the end and place this eye correctly in the bottom nock. Note that it seats properly. Inspect it carefully the first time, for if you accidentally bend the bow backwards, it likely will break. Push the upper loop high enough so that tension will hold it in place.

2. Now, stand with your feet comfortably apart, and grasping the bow backwards with your left hand, rest the bottom tip against the inside of your left foot. Lift your heel to keep the bow off the ground. Swivel your body to the right so that your right leg is straight and your left knee slightly bent.

3. Grasp the top loop string on either side of the bow

Standard method of bracing a bow. Note that lower tip does not rest directly on ground, and that bow is pressed against the body, not swung out in front.

with your thumb and forefinger. Keep your other fingers out of the way so that when you slide the string up to the nock (the next step) you won't pinch your fingers between bow and string. Bend your body slightly to the left at the waist.

4. O.K. Now comes the tough part. Read this first before proceeding: Push downward and forward with the heel of your right hand (partly by straightening your body at the waist) while you hold your left hand—pulling—against your right thigh. As the bow bends, your right fingers will niggle the string upwards until it slips into place in the nock. Keep the string taut so the lower loop doesn't un-nock.

5. When the string slips in place, inspect it to make sure, then glance down to the other end to see that the lower eye hasn't sneaked out. If anything is wrong, either fix it (still keeping the bow-bending pressure) or slip the top loop out, relax slowly, and start all over. (The biggest fault with beginners is that they let the bow swing too far away from the body.) If the bottom loop has become misaligned, a sudden release of pressure could twist the bow out of shape, or could pull the loop out of its groove, and the bow end might bury itself in your cheek, or worse, could break.

Wayne Aitken of Colt's Fire Arms demonstrates proper method of step-through bracing. Bow's center section is carried high on the rear, while pressure is applied to bow curves, not tips.

6. If all is well, swivel the bow around forward, still holding tight, and release the pressure. Check again to see that everything is as it should be. The pivot was to get you out of a possible line of fire.

To remove the string, reverse the procedure, allowing the eye to slip down onto the bow limb. One detail: Use only your forefinger to un-nock; keep your thumb wrapped around the bow, holding your grip so you don't slip. Let the bow straighten gradually.

As you get used to stringing, practice throwing your stringing-finger shoulder in front of your face to deflect a possible slipping bow.

Some archers flex their bows over the knee for added leverage, making sure that the knee is under the thick section rather than a flexing portion of the bow.

Step-through bracing is used on recurve bows of average and heavy weights, and on very heavy straight bows. It's easier than the standard method, you'll be happy to know, but if done improperly can twist your bow out of line. Some bowmen get the procedure *almost* right, and see no ill effect on the bow for months. By the time they realize what is wrong with their shooting, the bracing procedure has become well entrenched, and the bow has developed a permanent warp. What happens is that the wood (usually maple) ruptures, eventually allowing the string to jump off the bow when it is shot, but affecting arrow flight long before things reach that stage. It's said that step-through bracing has ruined more bows than any other single thing, with one exception: slamming trunk lids on bow ends. So—if at all possible, get an expert to supervise your first try.

1. Wrap a towel or sweat shirt around your left ankle. Later, you'll not need this, but for now, better guard against a sore shinbone.

2. Seat the string in the lower nock, then grasp the bow with your right hand toward the upper tip, holding the top end of the string with your left. With your right foot, step through, between the string and the bow.

3. Now the important part—adjustment of the bow. Slip the lower recurve over the front of your left shin (over the towel) and place the bow handle high across your rear. It's easier to use your thigh, but if you do, the upper limb will be bent more than the lower, and if the bow doesn't break, its cast may well eventually be thrown out of whack. (Some archers bend their left foot pigeon-toed and hook the top over their shoe, but most prefer the recurve around their instep.)

4. With the right hand, push forward on the curve of the limb sticking up under your arm. (Don't push on the tip.) Check to see that the lower limb is bending in a plane with the bow, not twisting out of shape. If you can see the lower nock, check it again to make sure the eye hasn't slipped. Lift the left foot slightly.

5. Now, with your left knee slightly bent, your right straight, steadily apply pressure forward with your right hand in the upper curve while pressing backward with your rump. With your left hand, slip the string loop into place

After bracing, eyes must be inspected to see that they are properly seated.

over the upper bow tip. Bending forward at the waist may help some. Be sure to push the upper limb straight forward, not twisted toward your body.

6. Before releasing the pressure make sure both eyes are seated, then slowly relax.

7. Hold the bow in front of you and sight down the string. If your gymnastics warped the bow, this check will spot it. If it is twisted, put one end between your calves and twist on the other. It should easily bend back in place.

As a final step in any bracing method, place one tip of the bow on top of your foot, and grasping the upper limb about midway up with your left hand, and the string about six inches from the serving with your right, pull the string and bow apart gently a couple of times. Do the same with the other end. This will cause the string to untwist a bit and to seat properly in the groove.

Chapter 8

STAND, NOCK, DRAW, RELEASE

H AND a bow and arrow to a person who has never before seen archery equipment and he'll probably stand facing the target, grasp the arrow between his thumb and forefinger, drag it toward his chest, and prematurely release it. This is the "natural" method. It's wrong.

In the first quarter of this century another type archer was prevalent, and sometimes you still run across him. He stood ramrod straight with heels nearly touching, chest out, belly in. He nocked, drew and soldierly loosed his arrows by the numbers. He too was wrong.

Wrong, it can be said, because neither of these guys hit with any regularity. The "natural" shooter has no frame of reference, can draw the same twice only by accident. The spit-and-polish tin soldier lacks consistency because he's probably off balance and his tightened muscles won't allow him to stand at attention through more than half a dozen ends.

Unfortunately, it's not so easy to say what's right. Watch a tournament or a first-class field exhibition and you'll see nearly as many styles as shooters. The only criteria a mentor can cite are those points used by the majority of consistently excellent bowmen.

The first time a new archer steps up to the shooting line with an arrow and bow in his hands, he faces a critical mo-

ment. This is the time when groundwork is laid for his archery future, for during this and the next half-dozen times on
the range he cements the largest building blocks of his
archery foundation.

As a beginner, years ago, I had nobody around to teach
me the essentials, so I figured things out for myself. A few
weeks later, just when I began congratulating myself on how
accurate I was getting, a local champ visited my backyard
range. He pointed out quite a few errors. One was my anchor
point, the place where the draw hand rests at full draw. I
was sticking my thumb into my cheek, with my hand out in
front of my face; my aim was about as accurate as if I were
rifle shooting with only the forward sight. Though I quickly
changed to a firmer anchor (to steady my "rear sight"), a
month later I still had not equaled my non-anchored score,
so entrenched was that original thumb-in-cheek habit.

The point of this rather drawn-out confessional is this:
When you learn a new technique—particularly one which
uses muscles in unaccustomed ways—try to do it right the
first few times, else the quickly learned bad habit will stick
even when enlightenment dawns.

So then, for the first few archery essentials: how-to techniques for the stance, nock, draw, hold, release and follow
through. (There's one obvious omission: aiming—so important that a separate chapter will be devoted to it.) Each step
must be mastered individually, and all coalesced into a
smoothly working whole.

The stance

Today, nearly all topnotch bowmen follow the "relaxed"
line—firm joints, but not taut; solid stance, but eased. The
legs, for example. Though locked knees and tightened thighs
form the most rigid base for the body, such tenseness (especially when carried out through the rest of the body) saps
strength quickly, and a tired archer is an inaccurate one.

In the semirelaxed stance the feet are at a comfortable distance apart (unspecified); toes are turned in, straight, or turned out, which ever seems most comfortable. Knees are neither bent, nor locked. Body weight should be evenly distributed. Spend a moment or two finding a comfortable stance. Note it, but don't worry about it. If this particular part of your form changes slightly, O.K.

The modern archer stands at a 90-degree angle from the line of flight, toes touching an imaginary line drawn out from the target center. This should not vary. Some archers make it a practice to kick toe marks into the ground so that they will be sure to return to the same place after each end.

One rather rare stance should be mentioned: the *oblique*. Few bowmen use it, but those who do are very vocal in its praise. In it, the right foot (for right-handers) is moved just over the center line, while the left is moved back and swiveled so that it points toward the target. The waist is twisted, weight rolled forward to the balls of the feet, the knees locked. Proponents of this rather awkward-feeling stance say that it prevents swaying, helps cut down the natural tendency to lean back during a long round, and allows the heavily muscled archer a chance to use his back power. It's a very tiring stance, however, requiring a high degree of concentration, when the archer could instead be concentrating on more important aspects. Experienced archers can experiment, but the oblique stance is not recommended for beginners.

Nocking

The object of nocking is simply to place the arrow nock on the string at the nocking place. It's not really very important how you get it there, just so the method is fast, requires as little movement as possible, and becomes such a habit that the act becomes automatic.

Here is a sequence followed by perhaps the majority of shooters; it seems to be about the most efficient, once you get used to it:

1. Stand on the shooting line (facing 90° from the target) holding your bow by the grip. Raise it more or less parallel to the ground in front of you, the top of the bow to the right, the arrow plate up, the string beneath your left forearm.

2. Draw an arrow from your quiver by grasping it by the nock between your thumb and forefinger, and flip it over onto the arrow rest.

3. Spin the nock between your thumb and finger until the cock feather (the odd one) is up. Most modern nocks have a ridge running down the side, in line with the cock feather, for nocking by feel. (The cock feather must stand out from the bow to avoid being ripped off).

4. Pull the nock down and back toward you so that the string enters the slot.

5. Slide the nock up or down on the string until it halts in the nocking place.

6. Pull back a bit and place the forefinger of the left hand on the arrow at the bow (the only time this finger does such a thing) so the tension of the string holds things in place while the right hand relaxes. Soon you'll run through the whole shebang without thinking about it.

Drawing

A multitude of string-holding grips have been used at one time or another—everything from the Sioux style (all four fingers and thumb pinch the string) to the Mongolian draw (the thumb pulls from inside the partly clenched fist). Today, with the exception of a few isolated nonconformists who use two or four fingers, the three-fingered draw is used almost universally in Western countries.

To use this draw, hold your half-cocked bow more or less horizontally in front of you with your left hand pointed down. With your right hand, reach under the string, palm up, and place your forefinger to the right of the nock, the middle and ring fingers to the left. At the start of the draw, the string crosses the fingers about a third of the way from the first knuckle crease to the tip; at full draw, the string has rolled out till it rests a third to half the way in from the fingertips—the correct placement whether the fingers are bare or protected by a tab or glove.

Ideally, the string hand during the draw is straight from the wrist to the middle knuckles. Fingers are held at right angles to the string and close together, snug against the arrow to make sure it doesn't slide out of nock. The string is drawn, not the arrow itself. The thumb does nothing; fold it into your palm and forget it. Same with the little finger.

As for the left arm, only two things need concern you: the elbow should be very slightly bent (hardly enough so you'd notice it, but enough to get away from locking), and the inside of the elbow (whatever that's called) should be swiveled somewhat out of the way, to prevent string slip.

To check your elbow-swivel, stand on the firing line with the bow (minus arrow) grasped loosely and hanging comfortably at your side. Your left arm probably will be slightly bent, though you *can* straighten it by stretching downward with your hand. Don't. Leave it relaxed. Look over your left shoulder at the target and bring the bow up horizontally. When it gets somewhere around shoulder height, start turning it vertically, using only your wrist and forearm. You probably won't be wholly successful, but it will do. Your forearm should now be out of the string path. (To show yourself the wrong method, swivel your elbow down under and around; now it's in the way of the string.)

While the bow is out there, tug the string. Your hand should be gripping the bow loosely with the string pressure pulling on the crotch made by the junction of your thumb and forefinger. If it presses on the heel of your hand, that's wrong, will lead to what is called "heeling"; the bow will tend to point skyward—and so will your shots.

The bow isn't grasped, it's rested against the hand. Some champion archers, in fact, use such a loose grip that their bows must be secured to their wrist by a thong, else the bow

Above: Underjaw anchor, primarily for target work. Below: Cheekbone or high anchor, ordinarily used in field archery.

Equipment, courtesy Colt

would fall to the ground when the arrow flies. The softer the grip, the less shock wave will be transmitted to the arm, and the smaller will be the automatic jerk the arm gives as the dynamic bow forces unwind. Imagine that the front of the bow is made of mushrooms; if you squeeze, it will squash. Instead of gripping the bow, "lean" against it. (A few bow grips, however, are so formed that you can't really tell what's pressing on what. If this is the case, keep the above in mind, but don't let it throw you.)

One other reason for a loose grip is that with a strong grip, an archer may tend to twist the bow to the side, causing the limbs to unwind in a plane other than that formed by the arrow-target line; in order to hit the target, the archer would have to shoot to the side.

With the bow still at arm's length, check yourself to see how you're lined up, or you might have an understanding friend read the following paragraphs aloud. First, your feet are comfortably apart at right angles to the target; your legs feel solid, but at ease. Nothing is turned toward the target but your head. Your hand, wrist, arm, shoulders, and chest are forming a more or less straight line out from the target. Your shoulders are level. Your head is upright.

O.K. Relax. You've got it. Time for the arrow.

Stand perhaps 5 yards from the target. (You should stay within 30 feet for your first 500 shots.) Nock the arrow, hold it in place and look sideways at the target, concentrating on the gold. Take a deep breath, raise your left arm, and swing the bow from horizontal to vertical as you pull back with the right hand (pull the string, not the arrow), until the arrow is aiming at the target, your right elbow has pulled back around your head and is pointing directly behind you, your hand is resting against your face. (Just where will be discussed five paragraphs hence. For now, pick a spot that seems right.)

As you near the end of your draw, note where the arrow point lies—probably two or three inches in front of your bow, assuming you are a beginner who hasn't yet developed the full draw of which you are capable. Beware of the natural temptation to bend your head forward to meet the string. Keep it upright, or it may lead to a short draw, lowering the arrow's trajectory.

Now gently relax your right hand muscles so that your fingers straighten out and the arrow flies away. If you got anywhere near the target, I'll buy you a beer.

You'll notice that no mention was made of which arm actually does the work—the right pulling or the left pushing. Neither was it suggested at which point this work should begin. The reason is that every person has his own method of doing it—that which feels best to him—and conformation to the ideas of a tutor might do more harm than good. Besides, I have no idea which of my own arms does the more work, nor can I say with certainty where this work is done. My arms stretch apart and the bow comes up. That's it.

A problem now, with, fortunately, an answer. Probably no beginning archer ever drew his first arrow that it didn't lift from the rest and float aimlessly off to the left. If this happened to you, the probable reason is that you got apprehensive. Afraid that you'd loose the arrow before you were ready, you curled your fingers more tightly around the string

—and the turning string (rightfully snug in the nock) simply picked up the arrow and swung it around. Frustrating. To guard against this, roll the string the other way—from the knuckle out. Don't worry about it; when your muscles become used to the strange position, you'll feel more secure and automatically compensate for a swinging arrow.

Now for the anchor point, the control of the nock at full draw, the single most difficult thing in all archery.

The arrow's point can easily be seen by the archer, but the nock must be controlled by feel. The anchor point takes care of two things directly and one indirectly. It controls the length of the draw, the vertical displacement of the arrow, and to a lesser extent, horizontal placement. Obviously, if these things aren't consistent you never can hope to drive two arrows into the gold with anything but luck.

The hand of a pro at full draw, so relaxed you wonder why the bow doesn't drop at release.

Generally speaking, anchor points can be divided into two categories: the underjaw, low, or target anchor, and the cheekbone, high or field anchor. The underjaw is used primarily in target archery—shooting at known distances often with the use of bow sights or other sighting aids. It seems to be somewhat easier for many beginners, and for some reason—there's much argument on this—most of the high-scoring target champions use the method. Essentially, the arrow nock is brought up under the chin.

The cheekbone or high anchor point, not surprisingly, is

at cheeckbone height. It is used extensively in hunting and field shooting at unknown distances, and is less likely to be used with bow sights. Hunters like it because the arrow is brought up nearer the eye, narrowing by almost 50 percent the angle formed by the eye-target line and the arrow-target line. And the flatter trajectory of hunting arrows (usually the bows are more powerful, distances shorter) obviates great discrepancies between target and point-of-aim. (This will be discussed at length in the chapter on aiming.) High scores on the target range, however, have been made with high-anchor positions; and clean kills in the field have been made with underjaw anchors.

If you are just beginning in the game, this is the time when you must make an anchor position choice, and this depends on which kind of archery you expect to do more of during the next couple of years—target or field.

If you figure target work will take up most of your time, you'll now decide on a low anchor point. No two faces are alike, and so no two underjaw anchor points are exactly the same. To find a good one for you, draw back the nocked arrow until the string rubs against the right side of your nose and passes over your lips. (Keep your teeth together.) You should be looking straight down the arrow with your right eye. If not, move the nock right or left. (For now, close your left eye if you want to, but don't get hooked on the habit.)

Almost invariably the untutored beginner shoots to the left of the target. The reason is that he draws the nock up pointed somewhere around his neck or ear. While the pile seems to point at the target, the feathers are headed somewhere off in right field. The arrow goes straight—off to the left.

When you find a place on your face which places the nock on some vertical plane of the eye-target line—when you look straight down the arrow to the target—move your hand up or down to find a spot that feels solid. Some archers draw to the corner of their mouth, others put a knuckle under a chin point, many pose a forefinger on a chin bone or put the heel of their hand on their Adam's apple.

Some archers use little *kisser* buttons (available at your archery store) to make sure they use the same anchor point each time. These rubber or plastic knobs slip over the string, are held between the teeth while the archer is sighting. Try a few winds of thread to see if you go for the idea.

If you expect to do a great deal of field archery, then your anchor point is farther back, higher, and off to the right. Some people use an upright thumb on the ear, others find a solid tooth or bone end best. (One bowman for years used a tooth felt through his cheek, then lost this anchor tooth. His score dropped overnight, didn't rise again until he located a wart under his chin that he could feel with his little finger.) You'll have to tilt your head over to the side a bit to compensate for this farther-away anchor, to bring your eye over the arrow. Use a mirror to make sure your head-tilting

Kisser button—a plastic or rubber knob that slips over the string—assures this man that his draw is correct. Archer is Hans Deutgen, former Swedish world champion. He's shooting an all-steel bow.

Courtesy, American Swedish News Exchange

hasn't thrown your whole form cockeyed. Don't, by the way, go too high. If you try to sight down the whole arrow your hand will be up too far for your muscles to control, and the pressure of your hand can distort your vision.

One thing more: Be sure your arrows are long enough for this farther-back method of drawing. Overdrawing can occur if you're used to an underjaw anchor and suddenly decide to try a cheekbone.

Anchor point established, you should be able to get a full draw without much trouble. Nevertheless, many amateurs have draws that vary—mainly toward the end of a session when fatigue forces them to come to something less than a full draw. As a hedge against letdown, common practice is to check the end of the point at each draw. A few archers draw little rings around their arrows near the point to indicate position. Such tricks are frowned on, however; the archer has too much else to think about than visual draw-checking. For the beginner, the aids sometimes help a bit.

A few archers draw almost to their anchor—say, an inch or so from it—then sight, and *then* complete the draw, followed by an immediate loose. This may work for a time, but usually the knack is suddenly lost and the scores plummet, never to be regained. It's a bad habit.

Another thing: It's not enough that the string cuts your face at the same place every time or that your hand rests in the same contour; a slight change in head placement can throw off your anchor point—drastically.

Holding

At full draw, before the arrow is loosed, everything comes to a halt. This *holding* period is an essential part of the shooting process, and probably is the most underrated step in the whole sequence. Even during pressure of the hunt, a hold of two seconds is considered about the minimum for accurate shooting. (If your bow isn't too heavy for you,

Courtesy, American Swedish News Exchange

↑
Old pro from Sweden just before release. Notice how the string pressure blanches his knuckles.

←
If necessary, the bow may be canted slightly to give an unencumbered view, as here demonstrated by Virginia Acquarro of the Daytona Beach (Fla.) Archery Association.

Daytona Beach
Resort Area photo

you should be able to hold a full draw for almost ten seconds without wavering.)

What happens during the hold? You quickly run through the rudiments—feet lined up? draw full? head positioned? anchor set? aim correct? You make double sure your pile isn't wobbling around out there. Then you let 'er fly.

If you can't hold the full draw for a protracted time, you probably will subconsciously ease up a bit and the arrow will start to creep forward in what is called *collapsing*. The farther forward it goes (a collapse of a quarter-inch has a marked effect), the lower on the target the arrow will hit. If you are a beginner and you find yourself collapsing at the end of a long round, don't be surprised; your muscles just haven't learned yet what to do. Nearly all first-try archers do most of the pulling with the upper-arm biceps, but after a few days, more of the work is automatically taken up by the powerful muscles of the shoulders, upper back, and chest. Soon these muscles synchronize, and suddenly one day you'll realize that all your attention is focused on aim and holding, that you've completely forgotten about bow weight. So startling might be the revelation you may even think that your bow has weakened.

Strength is the single most important advantage a prize-winner has over an amateur. As one world champion said, "Any archer who can put his sight in the middle of the gold, hold it there while relaxed and release at any time he wants can shoot fantastic scores."

If an experienced bowman begins to lose tension and starts collapsing, something is wrong. Either the bow is too heavy, the arrows too long, or the stance is off. A mirror tryout is called for, or a switch to arrows a half inch shorter, or a lighter bow—at least for practice.

Release (loose)

Letting go the string would seem to be one of the simplest aspects of the shooting cycle. Unfortunately, it's one of the trickiest. When a bow is drawn to its fullest and the arrow is poised, a tremendous amount of energy is stored up, all of it centered on and controlled by three tiny finger pads. And although some glib archers will tell you exactly what they do during the loose, listen to enough of them and you'll probably come to the conclusion that none of them knows just what goes on.

A couple of things *shouldn't* be done. Plucking is the most common. In this—or at least what the term has come to mean in archery parlance—the string hand moves back and to the right as the string is loosed, causing the arrow to misfire and land somewhere other than on the intended spot. (This also is called "flinching.") The whole thing would be O.K. if done exactly the same way each time, but few can get away with it.

Some bowmen claim they pluck the string on purpose as part of the loose. Maybe so, but it's doubtful. What probably happens is that the so-called pluckers are holding their finger ends at something wider than a right angle to the palm, and that if the string were gradually allowed to slide forward, the arrow could creep over the rest a fraction of an inch—the distance from the finger-pad string-holding crease to the tips—and the draw would thus be shortened. To compensate, these men likely draw their fingers back slightly as the string is sliding down the finger-pads, the result being that the string actually doesn't move until the tips are passed. Then when the tension is finally taken off the string, the hand automatically flies back a little (as the bow tends to travel forward) giving the *appearance* of a pluck.

A couple of other things to watch: Release the string by all three fingers simultaneously; don't let it slip off one, then bounce off the adjacent. Don't select an anchor point which allows the released string to flick off part of your face; you'll begin to flinch. Watch that one finger isn't doing all the work while the others ride free. (A blister on the finger means you're either making it do too much work or pinching the arrow nock.) Such faults often are difficult to detect. A good idea is to get a fellow archer to stand behind you occasionally for release inspection.

Follow Through

As the arrow is loosed the bow will fly forward a bit, the string hand and right shoulder automatically will move back. Don't fight it, but don't drop the hands either; keep in position until the arrow strikes the target. There are two reasons for this: 1) At release time the bowman is tired from straining to sustain the full draw. He has a tendency to relax just as the arrow is leaving the rest. If he doesn't make a conscious effort to stay in the firing position, he may move the bow before the arrow leaves, shattering accuracy. 2) If the arrow misses the mark widely, the cause is easier to pin down if the body is as close to the draw position as practical. This latter reason is particularly valid when the bowman is shooting at moving targets. (On the actual hunt, though, you'll be reaching for another arrow as the first one speeds on its way, so the true follow-through won't be practical.)

Final reminder: Once you have taken your initial stand, stay in your tracks until the end is completed.

Chapter 9

SIGHTING

ONE of the hottest controversies in archery today is the question of aiming. At one end of the spectrum are purists of the "bare-bow" school. They fancy themselves Indians, disdaining anything remotely resembling accuracy aids, including in some far-out cases, arrow rests and nocking points. At the other end of the continuum are those people so overloaded with automatic range-finding and battery-operated telescopic sighting devices that the next step would be an automatic bow-shooting machine. (And there have been those, too.) So bitter has the wrangle become in some quarters that the whole objective of bowmanship has been forgotten: hitting the target—whether it is a succession of diminishing circles or the heart of a moose.

Fortunately, the majority of bowmen have viewed this turmoil from the sidelines, and many of the top men have one foot firmly planted in each camp. One, for example, is Joe Thornton, a Cherokee Indian from Oklahoma who in 1962 broke all records at Oslo at the FITA International, the world championship. He hunts with one aiming style— so-called "instinctive"; and he shoots in tournaments with another—using a bow sight. Those two kinds of aiming plus the point-of-aim method cover 95 percent of the sighting methods used in the Western world today.

In the hunting or instinctive method, the bowman aims and shoots much as a rifleman would fire from the hip, with no conscious sighting reference other than the target. The point-of-aim man, on the other hand, hardly looks at the target. He uses a marker—a tuft of grass, a distant tree, a white ball placed on the ground—on which he lines up the arrowhead. The archer equipped with a bow sight steadies a bead on the gold and ignores everything else.

Of the three, the bow sight is by far the most accurate, the hunting method the most difficult. The point-of-aim (POA) style probably teaches the most to the inexperienced archer, and its rudiments are the most easily grasped. I'll suggest, then, that the beginner learn aiming technique of the POA, then advance either to the bow sight if he is concerned mostly with target shooting, or to the hunting technique if that is his wont.

First, though, a look at eyes. Particularly closed eyes. Should there be any? No. Not in aiming.

Nearly all people have what is called the master eye, the one that is sharpest, strongest, or which does the most work. To check yours, do the following: (Don't reason it out first, but do it quickly, without thinking.) Extend your arm with your thumb pointing upward, and with both eyes sight a distant object. Now close your left eye. If your thumb stayed in the line of sight, good. You'll have no trouble if you are right-handed. If your thumb seemed to jump over to the left when you closed your left eye, let's hope you're left-handed. Otherwise, you may run into some difficulty getting used to using your non-master eye as the master. However, if your right eye is *very* poor, you may have to close your left after all, or as some archers do, use a pair of glasses with the left lens covered. Or squint your left eye while you get things lined up, then open it before loosing. Or learn to shoot left-handed.

What's the difference? Keeping one eye closed is fatiguing, will cause facial muscle strain which inevitably will affect your accuracy. More important, though, is that by using only one eye your distance judgment will plummet, since perspective depends on binocular vision. Both eyes open gives a clearer picture of the target—especially in hunting, and particularly in the fall when game blends with foliage background.

Closely tied to binocular vision is judgment of trajectory. The principles are important to keep in mind, even though you put the knowledge to work only indirectly.

As soon as an arrow leaves a bow, gravity takes effect immediately, and the missile begins to fall toward the ground. If the arrow is pointing upward as it is loosed (almost always the case) it describes a parabola, a specific kind of curve dear to the hearts of mathematicians. The trajectory is never flat, but the heavier the bow, or the lighter the arrow, or the further the draw, the more nearly flat the curve. In other words, if you draw an arrow five feet from the ground and shoot it perfectly horizontally at a target also five feet from the ground you're not going to hit the exact center no matter how fast the arrow travels nor how close the target. You have to aim a bit higher. The same goes for a bullet, but a slug leaves the barrel with such a tremendous velocity that for several hundred yards, drop presents no problem.

The archer, however, is at a considerable disadvantage with his lighter equipment and slow missile speed (about 200 feet per second). He must compensate for this drop, else his arrow will dig earth before the target. If the point of the arrow can be compared with the front sight of a rifle, and the eye to the rear sight, this means that there is a rear elevation of somewhere between two and six inches or so, depending on whether a high or low anchor is used.

With any given man-bow combination (if the draw is constant) there is only one distance from the target at which the archer can sight over the point, see the gold, and hit it. With a 40-pound bow this range—called the point-blank distance—is about 80 yards. (For practical purposes a rifle's point-blank range is everything up to a couple hundred yards.) Closer than a bow's point-blank range the arrow is pointed so high that its trajectory will carry it over the target; farther, it will fall short.

Targets are set at point-blank ranges a disappointingly small percentage of the time. Therefore, the archer must compensate. And it's this compensation—whether done "instinctively" with hunting-style sighting, by point-of-aim, or by using bow sights—that all the sighting shouting is about.

Hunting-style sighting

This is the classical method of shooting, the technique used by the American Indian and almost everyone else until in the 1850's. In hunting style, with neither sight nor distance figuring, you just pull the arrow and shoot and hope that, because of the many scores of hours put into practicing, you will "instinctively" hit the target.

That word instinctive is debatable. Some unknown smart cookie thought it up and it's stuck fast, applying to anyone who shoots bare-bow (without a sight). It originated with the idea that throwing a stone is instinctive (it isn't—it's learned), and that if one has "good instincts," he can shoot a bow with no new-fangled gadgets or distance-judging tricks. To a certain extent this is true; some people have excellent timing or coordination between eyes, brain, and muscles, have above average judgment as to just how much the bow should be tilted to send the arrow *that* far. But there's little genuine instinct involved. Wayne L. Aitken, Southeast regional manager for Colt Fire Arms, says, "My definition of a truly instinctive archer is a guy who shoots with both eyes shut."

Truly instinctive or not, the champion bare-bowman doesn't estimate distances any more than a baseball player stops to figure how far he is from second. He throws by feel rather than by calculation, using abilities brought about through long practice—and when it counts, he can let his subconscious take over. So it is with a bare-bowman; his coordination is honed to such a razor edge that in the hunt he can raise his bow and fire while only half realizing what he's doing.

But there's lots of over-lap between hunting-style aiming and the use of sights or markers. Some of the best "instinctive" archers today use gadgets for target shooting, and the lessons learned on the target range carry over to the field.

Before real progress can be made the tyro archer must find out his faults—and using a sight for at least part of the training process takes out much of the guesswork. Then, after learning the fundamentals of estimating distances, he uses the information in the field, consciously or not.

Hunting-style aiming has distinct advantages. The hunter or roving archer is prepared to shoot over any distance, uphill or downhill, in a variety of positions and circumstances. Overhanging branches may necessitate leaning the bow, making sights nearly useless. And a bowman using this method can get his arrow off quicker than by any other. He must, for usually he has only a split second to make a sighting judgment. Besides, how do you pace off the distance to a flying pheasant? Further, between 92 percent and 94 percent of all hunters use instinctive aiming; although statistics can be misleading, the fact that such an overwhelming majority prefers this method year after year cannot be discounted.

On the other hand, hunting-style aiming has its disadvantages. Inaccuracy, for one. Because of this, many topflight bowhunters won't even draw if the game is more than 50 yards away. Although there have been a few instances of 100-yard kills, the national average is about 35 yards. So critical are long shots that an archer who (consciously or unconsciously) estimates a 50-yard range at 54 would have a twelve o'clock miss over the deer's back; if he got off another shot, re-estimating the range at 46 yards, the arrow would skittle under the animal's belly.

How, then, does one gain the rather remarkable ability of

hunting-style aiming? First of all, forget any conscious effort to estimate range in yards or feet. Few of us have this ability to any marked degree, but we do have the knack, strangely, to judge the arching flight of a missile. To demonstrate it, try this exercise. Select at random a tree some distance away. Pick up a rock and throw it, trying to strike the tree at the ground. Note where it hit. Now estimate the distance to the tree and pace it off. Unless you're a very remarkable individual, your guess wasn't within 20 percent. But chances are again that your rock came well within 5 percent.

To start shooting with a hunter's technique, get back a dozen paces from a target, draw and hold. Concentrate on the target center with both eyes open. If you are using a high anchor point (and if you're serious about this method, it's a good time to develop this anchor), tilt the bow to the right a bit to reveal more of the target. With your peripheral vision acknowledge your arrow point, but don't look directly at it. Without flicking your eye down, note also in a vague way that the arrow is in line, and that it has the right elevation. How? Guess. The vertical distance between the out-of-focus arrow point and the target will clue your brain as to how you're set up—the shorter the range the broader this distance.

Your first few shots will likely miss the target. But don't think about it. Just keep shooting. Sooner or later your brain will slip into gear; your inner computer will note what's wrong, add the necessary data, and program the calculations for your muscles.

At a specific range—about 70 or 80 yards for a hunting bow—the point will be exactly on target. Beyond this range, rarely used in the hunt, it will be above the target. This "space picture" is your rough guide. With practice, everything but the target will fade from your mind, and your innate ability to judge will take over. Gradually you'll feel more and more of those satisfying moments when your arrow arcs to perfect hits over completely unknown distances.

California's Marie Stotts, 1962 NFAA title holder, explains her instinctive technique this way: "I draw as I raise my bow. . . . My bow arm finds the target and stops. . . . I align the string and the arrow with the spot . . . then relax while holding [the bow] at arm's length and look at the target for several seconds, then relax the fingers while keeping the bow arm still until the arrow is in the target. . . . My eyes haven't left the target."

It's trickier to hit a moving object because you not only have to judge distance, but lead. This takes plenty of practice—starting well before the hunting season. Few suggestions really are worthwhile, but try this: Draw and aim behind the game, then swivel at the hips and bring your aim through the game to a point in front of it. Keep the bow moving as you loose. Naturally, the farther you are from the quarry and the faster its speed the more lead necessary. Fortunately, the archer—unlike the rifleman—can watch the course of his arrow as it speeds toward the target, and adjust his second shot accordingly. An important point is to keep the bow moving after release—assurance that you don't stop your swing prematurely. Watch an old-time bowhunter and you'll see that his follow-through swing will last until the arrow strikes home.

A particularly confusing bit of business for the nouveau bowhunter is hill shooting. This, too, should pretty much be left to on-the-spot judgment, but a couple of hints might help: Downhill shooting gives a flatter trajectory than you might imagine; compensate by aiming a little lower than usual. Ease upward on uphill shots. The reason is that when you shoot uphill you're fighting gravity more than when you fire horizontally. The arrow actually will take a little longer to go a given distance, and since the gravitational drop in the curve of the arrow's path is directly proportional to the time it's in free flight, it follows that on uphill shots the arc drop will be more pronounced, something for which there must be a compensating higher aim. The converse is true for downhill shots.

One more technique should be mentioned in connection with hunting-style aiming—the "variable anchor" type of sighting. This seems to be growing in popularity, especially for field competition use, but should be experimented with only by those with lots of experience in conventional techniques. The archer using variable anchor points has located five or six different anchors on his face, noting that a change in anchor of about one-finger width causes an approximate 10-yard change in cast. Coupled with several different anchors, a few experimenters have perfected even more variation by combining variable anchors with draw-finger-position changes—three fingers over the nock, three under, two above, or two below. This gives them virtually infinite placements for every distance from 10 to 80 yards. In effect, they shoot point-blank whatever the range. (Of course, with this method you have to estimate distances pretty accurately.)

Point-of-aim sighting

In field shooting, the whole object is simulation of the hunt. The archer works over a variety of terrains, shooting from unknown distances. In target archery the distances are known, and no thought at all is given to quick work. While in field and hunt shooting the bowman concentrates on the target and sees his arrowhead only incidentally, in the point-of-aim system he concentrates on the point, aiming not at the target, but at some object below or above it.

To try out the system, stand at a rather close range—say, 20 yards—and kick a couple of toe dents in the ground to mark your position. Draw fully until your arrow point appears to be in line and somewhere below the target. Note the place. Now ease your draw, walk over to that point, and mark it with some object, preferably of a light color. Tinfoil from a cigarette pack will do nicely; or better, stick a pencil through the bottom of the cigarette pack and shove this into the ground.

Now resume your position, draw fully, and align the marker so it appears to be resting atop the pile. Loose an end of six matched arrows. If they cluster high on the target, move the marker toward you a few feet; if low, move it back toward the target. Continue this juggling until the arrows cluster on the gold. If the arrows bunch to the right or left of center, recheck your form, and if all seems right, move your shooting position in the same direction as the grouping is off. Think of the marker as a swivel point; if your arrows are grouped to the left of the target center, move back along the shooting line.

Better than kick marks in the dirt are carry-along foot markers. Some archers tote a handful of white golf tees for this purpose. Others use large white buttons with staples of heavy-gauge wire running through. One man used large nails welded to the center of two silver dollars. Said it brought him luck. (He came out twenty-eighth out of thirty-two in the tournament in which I saw him compete.)

Permanent POA markers are handy, too, if you plan to use this system. Large archery-supply stores sell spike-mounted hardwood balls for a half dollar or so. Or you can make your own: Glue a golf ball onto a tee. (Don't, by the way, hammer a spike into a golf ball; the highly compressed liquid center might explode.) Some archers use screwdrivers with the tops pointed white. In an emergency, use the feather end of a broken arrow.

For a permanent guide to POA locations, you'll need a range finder—a sighting stick with various distances noted on it, a relief from the burden of finding POA by trial and error. First get a dowel or a flat, thin piece of wood about six inches long. Something the size and shape of a tongue depressor would be ideal, but a light-colored pencil will do. Cut a V-shaped wedge in the end, and either cut two more V's on each side about a half inch from the end or bore a hole through the stick. Through this hole or around the V-shaped collar, tie a length of string, then holding the stick at arm's length in front of you, stretch the string to your nose. At this point attach a small button—to the string.

Whenever you place the button between your teeth and hold the stick at the taut-string distance, the length from your eye to the stick will be the same, providing your eye-to-tooth distance remains constant. (Another method is to bore a small hole near the top of the stick to receive the point of an arrow, the nock of which is rested on the chin.)

To calibrate your range-finder stick, measure 10 yards from the target and locate the POA by trial and error. Holding the stick so that the gold rests exactly in the top V, move your thumb up until its tip coincides with the POA marker. Mark this point on the stick. Relax a moment, then line things up again to make sure you're right. Do the same for 20 and 30 yards. The marks should be equidistant. Additional marks up to about 60 can be added without your having to go through the trial and error business. A coat of varnish or spray-on plastic will make the marks permanent.

To find future POA placement points, sight over the range finder, then flick your eyes to the appropriate mark, and keeping your eye on that ground point, walk out and plant your marker.

Heavy wind may throw things off. Wind from the back speeds the arrow, gives it less time to fall, causes it to strike high. The converse is true for a head wind. Side wind, too, must be adjusted for.

Bow sights

Unlike the archer who uses POA, the bow-sight man ignores the arrow, concentrates instead on superimposing a tiny bead or cross hairs sticking out from his bow, over the bull's-eye. Archers using bow sights have won every major tournament in both field and target competition—despite the fact that sights are relatively new in the history of archery.

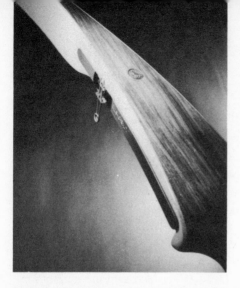

Typical inexpensive sight—this one the Line-O-Sight by Hoyt—is installed on bow with attached adhesive. Peephole slides in and out for windage, up and down for yardage.

Another inexpensive p e e p sight, in use.

They may be very complicated, consisting of telescopes, light beams, and prisms, and can cost up to $85 or more. Or they may be very simple—a matchstick hooked onto the bow with a rubber band. The majority of nontelescopic sights cost somewhere around $4. Essentially, a sight is some sort of reference point on the upper limb of the bow, just above the grip, adjustable up or down for distance and crosswise for wind. You line it up with the target, making, in effect, every range point-blank.

The sight usually does not tell the archer how far he is from the target (a very few models do); he has to figure that, and if his distance judgment is inaccurate, he's not much better off in the field or on an unfamiliar field course than the bare-bowman.

The simplest kind—but not very effective—consists of a series of ink dots on the belly of the bow, with distances, found by trial and error, lettered beside. Better homemade kind is a strip of ⅛-inch balsa wood about seven inches long, cemented to either the back or the belly and lined up with the edge of the bow nearest the arrow. The back is better, but if the belly is flat, it's easier to place it there. Over the balsa run a strip of adhesive tape, and stick a straight pin dipped in India ink between it and the balsa. Adjust the pin so that it sticks out somewhere above your arrow. By trial and error the correct sticking-places are found for various distances (multiples of ten yards for example) and marked permanently on the adhesive strip. Left-right adjustments are taken care of by pulling or pushing the pin. Except for minor changes for humidity, string tautness, and temperature, this simple bow sight is remarkably accurate.

One warning: Before calibrating any bow sight, be sure your form is as perfect as you can make it; don't set the sight to compensate for your mistakes. Next week if you consistently group at the target edge and everything with your sight seems O.K., you'll know that something in your style has changed in the meantime.

A big new thing in sights is telescopic models. Manufacturers claim that correctly used, well-made telescopic sights push scores of all classes of archers up 20 percent or more Though there are a variety of vari-priced models on the market, a typical one is made by SKA Scope Mount, Inc., of Spokane, selling for about $65 complete. Windage and elevation adjustments are accurate to 3 inches at 100 yards, and with a 30-pound bow, the prism allows the scope to be used anywhere up to 120 yards without sliding the sight up or down on the bow. Added features: The scope disconnects from the mount with a thumb screw, can be switched from one bow to another, and is guaranteed for 20 years. Says John P. Everett, editor of *TAM—The Archers' Magazine:* "There's been a lot of thought, archer thought, in the production of this SKA. . . .There's nothing perfect made by man, but this marriage is almost made in heaven from the looks of it!"

Good as they are, sights do present a couple of disadvantages. Among them: 1) The habitual sight user doesn't notice his arrow pile, and so he more easily overdraws or underdraws. 2) At long range the pile may intrude on the archer's vision. And with light bows used at great distances, the sight will come so close to the arrow that the feathers smack it. (This can be rectified by prismatic sights.) 3) Bow sight users have a tendency to concentrate on aiming to such a degree that their form is forgotten. Scope makers, however, insist that the opposite is true, that when you are doing something wrong the scope indicates it. 4) A bow sight user may become so used to his sight that he can't switch back again to another method. If he decides to hunt, very few animals will accommodate him by standing still while he figures the distance. 5) Some elaborate sights add considerable weight to the bow. This often is an advantage, however; added weight can give stability. 6) It takes a good man to estimate target distances closely enough to take full advantage of his sight when shooting at unknown ranges. (For $10 or so, though, you can buy a prismatic range finder operating on the parallax principle. Accuracy varies considerably, so before you buy, check with a tape measure.)

A commonly heard statement from those who are bare-bow advocates is that they *couldn't* use a bow sight to hunt —too tough trying to get the range on a moving target. This is nonsense. Nobody does. A sight user on the hunt knows that he probably will shoot at, say, between 25 and 55 yards (depending on terrain and game type). He sets his sights at 40 yards, and when he sees the quarry, allows for the different distance. Just like a bare-bow hunter—but with an aid. One California bow-sight hunter goes a step farther: He uses a sight with five pins set at 20 to 60 yards. No matter what the range, one of these pins is always close.

One more bow sight should be mentioned: the rear sight, used by former World Champion Joe Thornton. A few turns of black thread are wrapped around the bowstring, and he lines this up just to the right of the tip of his conventional sight. Simple enough to try, so give it a whirl.

SKA Scope Mount described in text.

World Champion (1959 and 1960) Jim Caspers sights with another telescopic bowsight, this one the Stiennon, developed by Norland Associates.

Chapter 10

WHAT'S WRONG?

FOR two days he hadn't seen a thing, and his long hunting weekend in Maine was about to run out. Suddenly, just before dark a giant buck crashed through the clearing where the archer was hiding. The animal ran straight toward him. "I had my bow ready in plenty of time," he told me later. "The arrow was already in the string and all I had to do was sight and shoot. But my hands wouldn't work. The broadhead swung off the arrow rest, my parka sleeve wrapped around the string, and suddenly I wasn't even sure I was pulling with the right hand.

"Well, when this buck came running up to me, I got so excited that I jumped up on a stump and hit him with my bow as he ran by."

Ridiculous. But true. Things *can* foul up that way; when the heat's on, you can go to pieces.

Usually it doesn't happen so dramatically—this complete loss of head at the moment of climax, this "buck fever," as it's called. Next time, you'll get the venison to the freezer. No worry.

Really worry-worthy is a similar ailment that appears primarily during tournaments—and the bigger the tournament and higher the pressure, the bigger the problem. Archers in various parts of the country may have their own pet names

for it—"pressure lock," "IT," "gold fever," "Targetitis," "freez-
ing," "target panic," even "thwack"—but simply, it's nerves.
You concentrate so hard, think so critically about each step,
that your body tenses in a semi freeze-up. This near panic
under tournament pressure comes from your body's pumping
adrenalin—instant energy—into your bloodstream in preparation for some massive effort. Under other circumstances—
100-yard dash, broad jump, a good fight—it's beneficial. But
in archery, it's disastrous. Tenseness may change your release
to a pluck, cause your bow hand to jerk, make your eye
flicker. Likeliest of all, tenseness may make you snap shoot.

Under tournament pressure, the average archer draws a
bead on a target, slowly swings over to the gold, glides past
it. But the arrow has gone. Almost subconsciously it was
loosed as the sight swept over the gold. The eye determined
loosing time, not the brain. And that's wrong.

A champion, on the other hand, concentrates on *not* loosing the arrow during that first sweep. Knowing that the
sight isn't going to stay in the gold, he waits until the sight
sweeps out, comes back, steadies down in the middle. He
holds the full draw until that sight stays exactly in the center
of the gold, hardly moving, nice and settled, then he lets
her go. No snap shoot.

To get rid of snap shooting and whatever else ails at high-
stake tourneys, archers have evolved all sorts of relaxation
techniques. Here are a few you might try.

. . . Every so often, slump, run in place, stretch, yawn,
throw your hands about. Fellow archers may wonder, but
higher scores are worth the stares. Object is to consciously
un-tense, to stretch those muscles, stimulate circulation,
work out any contraction.

. . . More appealing perhaps: Stretch out in the grass, stare
at a passing cloud, and tell each part of your body—feet,
calves, kneecaps, thighs, all the way up—to relax, to go limp,
to let the tension drain. Five minutes and (if it works) you'll
feel as though you've had an hour's sleep.

. . . Or you can try gadgets—a kisser button, bow-sling, clicker, offbeat finger tabs. They may not actually help, but involved with a gadget you might be somewhat distracted from your stage fright.

. . . If all else fails to break that knotted-up feeling, change hands and shoot a few arrows "other-handed." It'll feel terribly awkward, but when you switch back again the at-home feeling will be so pleasurable you may forget all about being tense. Or you might try shooting a couple of times with someone else's bow.

Best thing, say some top archers, is to develop a don't-give-a-damn attitude. This must be backed up with plenty of practice, though—so much that the whole shooting sequence becomes automatic. Next time you watch a champion shooter, study him carefully. Chances are he's the coolest one on the field. He acts deliberately and positively, but unemotionally. If he makes a wild shot, he looks disgusted, snorts, grins, or whatever, but he does it quickly, closes the door on it, immediately goes to the next shot.

When you're on the spot, say to yourself: "To hell with it; I have more important things to worry about than a silly game." You won't convince yourself, but it may help.

In Oriental countries, particularly Japan, archery is used not only to train the body, but the mind. At least one book has been written about archery as a stepping-stone to religion: *Zen in the Art of Archery,* by Eugene Herrigel, a German philosopher who took up archery in Japan to "obtain an understanding of Zen." Among Zen-oriented archers, the object isn't to hit the mark, but to shoot the arrow correctly; if the latter is successfully accomplished, the former follows automatically.

Preparation for correct shooting in some archery circles borders on autohypnosis. The shooter concentrates before a big meet on just what he's going to do; he visualizes himself standing firmly, drawing smoothly and carefully, holding evenly and centering without a quaver, loosing smoothly, and finally standing in a relaxed follow-through position while he watches the arrow arc to the mark.

In Zen, each step has its own "definition." For example, the release is compared with a leaf so weighted with snow that it slowly bends downward, finally allowing the burden gently to slide away.

Such visualization may work for some, but most of us are too much of the Western world. Better idea for Americans is to learn each part of the shooting cycle so well that all fit neatly together, turning the archer into a well-oiled shooting machine.

When you've passed the beginning stages of archery and start to feel that you're getting pretty good (usually a year to 18 months after you've started) it often happens that your score reaches a plateau, or even begins to edge downhill a bit. Chances are you're letting down somewhere along the path. (Incidentally, I used to know an archer in Cincinnati who every spring—tackle in hand—would uproot his wife's full-length dressing mirror from the bedroom and tote the thing to the backyard. There, in front of it, to the amusement of neighbors, he would perform an almost ritualistic archers ballet while he oiled up his rusty joints. Never did learn to shoot very well, though.)

Anyway, to help find out where you are falling down (assuming that your tackle is of the right kind and still in top shape), go through a few shooting cycles, checking the following points; they're the ones most likely to throw off an experienced bowman:

STANCE: Firm and balanced? Knees tight but not straining? Hips straight, not twisted?

NOCK: Not being squeezed? Nocking point in correct position? Index guide toward you? (Have someone stand behind you as you shoot; if the arrow tail drops or kicks up, your nocking point is likely too high or low.)

DRAW: Bow hand relaxed, palm open? Body swayless? Head upright with shoulders straight? Arm going straight back? String on balls of fingers with fingers straight? *Full* draw?

AIM AND HOLD: Both eyes open? Muscles not overtense? No premature release? Bow vertical or at normal cant? Concentrating on *center* of gold? Teeth together? Steadied down before release?

RELEASE: Smooth, with no pluck? Drawing hand in close? No right or left swing to bow hand?

FOLLOW-THROUGH: Eye on target, not the arrow? (Try thinking the word "statue," then posing until the arrow strikes.)

Sometimes the cluster of your hits suggests major faults. If you're shooting consistently to the sides or over or under the gold, check the following list:

ARROWS GROUP TO THE LEFT

1. *Jerky release.* This is the most likely problem. What happens is that you properly anchored and aimed, then at the moment of release plucked the hand back and to the right. Remedy: relax.

2. *Flinching*—caused by thwacking your arm with the string. Or maybe you have sore release fingers. Use a more protective arm guard and finger tab or tips.

3. *Bow strangle.* You may not realize it, but you could be holding the bow so hard that on release it is thrown out of line. Again, relax.

4. *Bow arm drop* on release, causing a seven o'clock cluster. Think about it and your arm will be apt to stay up.

5. *Sighting with the wrong eye.* Aw, come on.

6. *Side wind.* Compensate.

7. *Wrinkle in T-shirt* interfering with string. If this happens often, invest in a leather chest guard.

8. *Too stiff arrows.* Blame the arrows only after you've cleared yourself. Then only after you've let another archer try them out with your bow.

ARROWS GROUP TO THE RIGHT

1. *Bow-hand trouble.* Again. Make sure the bow seems to sink into the hand, that the hand doesn't seem to be pushing the bow away. Try using a bow strap and such a light grip that the bow falls toward the ground.

2. *Anchor moved to the left.* Not really very likely. Maybe you jerked back and inward, indicated by a one- or two-o'clock cluster.

3. *Bow tilt,* especially easy in hilly country. A good remedy is a small spirit level affixed to the handle riser.

4. *Draw-hand trouble.* Check to see that you aren't holding the string too far back on your draw fingers.

5. *Side wind.* Allow for it.

6. *Arrows too limber.* Again, get someone else to test the arrows on your bow before you blame the shafts.

OVERSHOOTING OR UNDERSHOOTING

1. *Faulty anchor,* which you inadvertently may have changed. With an underchin anchor, for example, an open mouth can make arrows shoot high. Look in a mirror.

2. *Faulty release.* Plucking with the right hand and pressing with the bow hand can cause over- or under-shooting. To test, hold the right hand extra still; consciously loosen the left, hold that follow-through a ridiculously long time.

3. *Mechanical trouble.* Arrows the wrong length, fistmele incorrect, sight slipped. Check the whole business.

4. *Overdraw,* producing flatter trajectory, higher grouping. Measure arrow length and note where the pile lies on the ledge.

5. *Collapsing*—allowing your anchor to slip forward, leading to low grouping. You've been shooting too hard. Rest.

Practice makes perfect. I once knew an archer who made it a point to shoot every day. On weekends he shot from morning to night, hundreds of arrows a day. This went on for months. But his score stayed about average; he never rose to the top echelon. Practice *did* make perfect; constant repetition of this guy's bad habits entrenched them so firmly that he made his mistakes perfectly, and it was almost impossible finally for him to wrench free.

But he did. Acting on the advice of a golf enthusiast, he went to a professional. The pro worked him over, straightened out a few minor things that the archer would have never found by himself. His score rose.

Oddly, the best thing about a really good coach is that he is less thorough than your friends, merely checking the high spots, seeing that you're doing such elementary things as holding the bow correctly, drawing right, sighting the way you should. Friends often offer too much advice. Still, a checkover by your fellow club members should be your first step.

And if you haven't yet joined a club, this is a good time. The U.S. boasts between 3,000 and 4,000 archery clubs—target, field, and combination, along with a smattering of such specialized groups as crossbow and flight. Almost all top archers are active club members. The reason is twofold: on the one hand a clubman ordinarily shoots more arrows during the year—the facilities are there; and on the other, through discussions—cross-fertilization of ideas—members simply are better informed about technique, equipment, and themselves.

Back to poor scores again—here's another reason, this one advanced by Lawrence C. Repucci, staff psychologist for Dow Chemical Company. Dr. Repucci claims that the reason snap shooters snap shoot is "a subconscious resistance to perfection"; they don't want to get a better score. According to Dr. Repucci, the archer's "internal logic" goes something like this: "If I get to be a good archer then I will be expected to get better. But to get better means that I will get more deeply involved in archery. But I don't want to get more deeply involved . . . therefore I will not get better." So theorizes Dr. Repucci. He indicates that if the snap shooter realizes *why* he is snap shooting, he'll no longer snap shoot. So you are informed.

At any rate, to be a really great champion, an archer must be either extremely intelligent or exceptionally dumb. Either he has to be so dumb he follows instructions without thinking things out for himself (and changing them for the worse) or must be so smart he figures things out correctly.

Chapter 11

DYNAMICS OF THE BOW
AND ARROW

MAN used the bow for a thousand years before he began to understand it. Through the ages he gradually developed gear adequate for his needs, but with a few notable exceptions (Turkish flight bows, for instance), the vast majority of archery equipment was terrible.

American Indians, for example, were lousy shots—not because their technique was necessarily poor, but because their equipment was close to hopeless. Hand-hewn bows of ash and yew coupled with arrows on which feathers were tied with sinew were little better than slingshots. An Indian had to sneak up to within 10 yards to hope for a hit.

The famed longbows of English armies were amazingly inaccurate, so far as we can tell today. No matter; the object wasn't to pick off individual soldiers, but to fill the air with volleys of arrows, some of which would hopefully land on the enemy.

The bows of Robin Hood and others of legendary fame may or may not have been of top quality. Perhaps they were, but more likely the bowmen lived so intimately with their equipment that skill made up for poor tackle.

It wasn't until engineers and physicists became interested in archery as a hobby that significant progress was made in discovering what really happens when an arrow is loosed.

Micrometers, slide rules, strain gauges, high-speed cameras and a multitude of other instruments gave bowyers data to put to work. As a result, all but a few of today's cheaper bows are technically far superior in design to the best of yesteryear.

Modern bows excell in many ways. One of the most dramatic is cast, or shooting power. Two principal factors are responsible: composition and design. Both have undergone dramatic changes in modern times, and bow makers are constantly experimenting with radical makeups and new materials to beat the competition. And because bows are individually purchased rather than being doled out by army quartermasters, highest standards are necessary. So bows keep on getting better, despite the insistence of traditionalists who say that straight bows, or yew bows, or those fashioned from the wood of ninteenth-century headboards are best.

Modern bows are made of a variety of materials; we have steel bows, wood bows, aluminum bows, a few experimental magnesium bows, and a whole raft of plastic and plastic-wood combinations. The newer materials have properties old bows could never challenge. Analysis of bow action shows why. When a bow is bent, it stores energy through two principal stresses, straining to return to the unbent position. The back stretches, storing energy through tension, and the belly shortens, squeezes together, storing energy through dynamic compression. Down the center lies a thin zone of inertness.

When a bow is loosed, it snaps back to the relaxed position with a speed depending in part on the stiffness, the ability of the bow materials to resist this stretching and compressing. The best material yet found for this snapback is high-tensile, high-compression fiberglass, a web of hairlike fibers of glass encapsulated in a plastic resin binder, of a formula especially designed for bows.

Most top quality bows are now made of plastic and wood laminate—the plastic on the belly and back, the wood forming the center core. The fiberglass provides nearly 90 percent of the power, while the wood core acts as an energy absorber, cushioning the shock wave of the loosed bow so it isn't passed on to the bow hand.

Another advantage to a composite bow is that the energy used to draw it is more fully stored than in all-wood bows; only a very small amount is lost—5 percent at most—largely through heat. The usable shooting power of a yew bow, on the other hand, might be only 80 percent of that required to pull it to the anchor position.

Bows best in theory work out best in practice, too. Interesting to note is this statistic from the 1962 National Field Archery Association sampling of big game taken during the year. Kills in the survey were made by 870 laminated glass bows, 31 all-fiberglass bows, and only 2 wood bows. None with metal bows.

Bow design can be classified under three main headings: straight, working recurve, and static recurve. (Any of these can also be a *reflex* bow—when unstrung it bends "backwords" a bit.)

STRAIGHT bows are the bows of old. The weight of a good straight bow builds smoothly over the entire draw. The string reaches its highest speed a fraction of an inch from the fingers, then decreases steadily as it nears the relaxed position. Additional weight in a straight bow is achieved either by 1) shortening the bow so that it bends more sharply with the draw, 2) adding to its thickness, or 3) increasing its width. Length and stiffness are almost exactly inversely proportional; increase a bow's length by 20 percent (assuming the size is constant throughout its length), and the stiffness should drop by 20 percent. Width varies directly with the draw weight; double the width of a straight bow and the stiffness doubles. But double the *thickness* and you cube stiffness.

Due to design simplicity, straight bows are unsurpassed in stability and dependability. But they fall down when compared with other styles in cast produced per given draw weight. To approach the cast of a fairly heavy working recurve bow, a straight bow would have to be so heavy you couldn't pull it back. And this is the reason that straight bows have pretty much died out among modern archers.

THE WORKING RECURVE bow was a major advance in bow technology. A conventional working recurve is more or less a short, straight bow, with limb extensions that sweep forward in smooth curves. When drawn, it feels like a heavy-pulling straight bow until the string is pulled back far enough to round the recurve bends and draw directly on the tips. Then the bow often seems actually to "soften" because the draw weight increases at a lower rate as the two miniature bows at the end of the limbs unbend. (Due to design modifications, this effect is difficult to detect in many modern bows. Actually, the limbs are so formed that everything unbends at once.)

As the working recurve bow is loosed, the string leaves the hand with about as much acceleration as with the straight bow. But when the tips have returned to their relaxed position, the string is considerably shortened. Its speed increases tremendously, exerting a final fling to the arrow, greatly increasing the cast.

For a given weight, the working recurve produces the greatest cast of any style. On the other end of the spectrum is a straight bow which has taken on a "set" that remains "bow-shaped" even when unstrung, often due to having been left strung for some time, or simply to its being an old, worn-out bow.

STATIC RECURVE bows are similar to working recurves, but instead of the tips curving forward in two tiny reverse bows, static limbs point forward abruptly; the bow looks as though its tips are broken. These ends are rigid, and unlike working recurve limbs, unbend hardly at all. The function of these tips is to make a long bow out of short one—to give long-bow drawing characteristics with short-bow power.

Though a short bow gives plenty of speed, it's difficult to draw, and because of the sharp angle of the string at full draw, has a tendency to pinch the fingers, making difficult a smooth release. With recurve ends added, drawing leverage is increased, the bow becomes easier to pull, the string angle larger. But the bow acts essentially as though the ends aren't there.

The trouble with the static recurve is that it has a poorer tiller (smoothness of letdown) than straight bows, a less sprightly cast than the working recurve. You don't see many of them anymore.

Many archers are unaware of a major change in limb cross section. Ask an archer to sketch the cross section of his bow limb, and chances are he'll draw an oval with a flat bottom. When he checks his bow he'll likely be surprised to see that actually it is a slightly round-cornered rectangle—maybe 1½ inches wide and 3/16 of an inch thick. The rounded-belly or "stacked" design was used almost exclusively until about the time architects began to utilize cantilever construction in buildings. Some unknown flexible-minded bow designer saw a similarity here, began to think of the bow as a pair of cantilevers resting on a common support (the hand) with equal loads (string eyes) at the tips. Borrowing building constructors' experiences, bow builders found that the most effective bow limb design has a constant thickness with a wide section at the handle gradually decreasing in width toward the tips. This allows the bow to bend more at the tips than toward the handle. This refined, constant-thickness, rectangular-sectioned bow limb design (particularly effective made from fiberglass laminate) has almost completely supplanted the older type. With it, the bow length can be shortened up to 20 percent with less danger of breakage.

Comes now a question that puzzled archers until the mid-1930's, a quandary aptly labeled "Archers' Paradox" by Dr. Robert P. Elmer, dean of American archery writers: Why does the arrow hit the target when all logic says it should strike far to the left?

All our lives we use the arrow to symbolize direction of travel—signposts at road junctions, weather vanes, force-direction signs in physics diagrams. But often the direction an archery arrow is pointing has little bearing on its flight. Says Walt Anderson, Omaha archery-physicist, "At times it would be better if we thought of the arrow as a small lead ball which is being thrust forward by the bowstring. We could then visualize that this projectile would travel in the direction the bowstring sent it."

The arrow is to the left of the center of the bow, and while at full draw the offset angle is very narrow, it becomes increasingly wider as the arrow and string are let down. At the "undrawn" point, the place at which the arrow leaves the string, the arrow aims for the left—some 14 feet, in fact, if a one-inch-wide bow is sighted on a 60-yard target. (To see this, nock an arrow and sight through the string to the center of the bow.)

You don't have to aim 14 feet to the right to hit the target, of course, but why, nobody knew. A whole raft of early theories were advanced to explain the oddity. The most widely accepted hypothesis was that the inertia or mass of the arrow actually pushes the bow handle out of the way, clearing a straight path toward the target. In 1924, Steward Edward White of Burlingame, Calif., built himself a shooting machine, a rack that would hold a bow rigid, and a hook to draw and loose the string. In a series of experiments, he almost proved this theory correct. With no lateral bow movement allowed, arrows did indeed shoot to the left. But not quite far enough leftward wholly to confirm the theory.

A few years later Dr. Elmer, dissatisfied with White's technique, decided to re-do the experiment. He built a similar shooting machine, and using a stiff hunting arrow found that his results confirmed the previous findings. Then he tried rather weak-spined target arrows, and to his astonishment found that they hit the target right on the nose. Then he selected his heaviest bow, fitted it with his lightest arrows, and reported this. ". . . The lighter arrows became like the good man who stands up so straight he bends over backward. They actually flew far to the *right* of the direction of aim." His conclusion (since confirmed): The arrow bends around the bow, with the pushing-out-of-the-way an additional factor.

It took the ultra-high-speed camera of Dr. Clarence N. Hickman to satisfy skeptics. Shooting slow-motion movies at 6,000 frames a second, Dr. Hickman proved that the following sequence describes the beginning of the flight of a correctly spined arrow in a well-designed bow:

1. At full draw the arrow shaft is pointing straight at the target; the string, left side of the bow, and the target are all lined up.

2. Immediately after the loose the string slips to the left as it slides off the fingers.

3. A fraction of an inch later it snaps back to the right, pulling toward the center of the bow. This action jerks the point to the left as it deflects off the bow.

4. As the arrow nears the one-third mark on its journey down the bow, it buckles even more, due to the pressure of the string and its flexibility—so much that the shaft pushes the arrow rest slightly right. Then suddenly it "bounces" away from the arrow rest (though no additional pressure is exerted on the rest) an eighth of an inch or so, never to touch it again.

5. The inertia of the arrow's pile resists the leftward swingout, but the center arrow portion doesn't. As a result,

the point heads around toward the bow front, causing the arrow to snake back around the arrow rest.

6. When the arrow leaves the string (which has been dragging the nock to the right, toward the bow), the nock reacts violently, snapping to the left. The point, meantime, has passed to the right of the original line-of-sight, but as a reaction to the nock snap, it begins to slop back left again, so that as the feathers whisk by the bow, the point is back in line with the flight plan. (English archers of four centuries ago, incidentally, believed that it was necessary for the nock to strike the bow in order that it be slapped back into straight flight. Today's archers refuse to tolerate a bow that allows nock sideswipe.)

7. As the feather end leaves the bow, it whips back in line and stays there pretty much, while the arrow's center portion bends to the right.

8. The arrow straightens out—and the center continues bending to the left. But not quite so much as before. Then back right again and so on, head and tail keeping pretty much in line while the center portion of the arrow vibrates back and forth, each wobble slightly less than the one before. It probably is still wobbling, albeit imperceptibly, as it strikes the target.

An arrow must be spined correctly to oscillate at just the right frequency to whip around the bow. If it is too stiff for the bow weight, it strikes to the left of the gold; if too weak, it will snake around the bow too much, and tend to travel too far to the right. If extremely weak for the bow, it will buckle as it bends around, permanently rupturing the fibers and warping the arrow or breaking completely.

Although bow weight is a major consideration in selecting the correct spine, it is not the only one. More important is the speed at which the bow unbends. (These two factors are most often parallel, but not always.) Therefore, if you find your arrows grouping to the left of center, they may be too strongly spined, despite what the bow-weight arrow-spine tables say. If arrows tend to head right, try stiffer spines.

Another thing that affects arrows' flight is the distance of the arrow rest from the center of the bow. A bow with no cut-in rest requires a weaker-spined arrow so the shaft can whip around the hemisphere of the bow. The more deeply cut the rest, the less spine needed, all other things being equal. An exact center rest, however, is not efficient, according to the majority of archery engineers. The pressures brought to bear on an arrow as it starts its flight are so great that it's going to bend anyway (beginning with off-finger flip), and without a bow to bend around, one never knows just what directions the undulations would take; the flight would be almost completely unpredictable. So-called center-shot bows are not (at least the ones that work); the arrow rest actually is about an eighth of an inch to the left of dead center—enough to impart a slight wobble in the right plane.

As the string flips off the fingers, the point of the arrow tends to lift upward between ⅛ and ¼ of an inch from the arrow rest—ample reason for placing the nocking point an eighth-inch up on the string: so the nock and point are directly in line as the arrow starts its journey.

If nocked too low on the string, the arrow is forced to ride up and over the rest. This intensifies its normal vertical oscillations (leads to wildly varying casts) which, so far as is known, perform no useful function (unlike horizontal motion which tends to stabilize an arrow's flight).

Some up-and-down vibration is inevitable. Two factors are responsible: 1) The bow hand is *below* the arrow flight line; when the arrow is released, the forces pull it at a slight tangent, imparting a vertical vibration. 2) "String Slack"; in a three-fingered draw, the apex of the string's V comes not at the nock, but at the center finger, a half inch or so below the nock. At release this V must snap from the finger to the nock; this quick shift causes a momentary slack in the string, resulting in strong vibrations which are passed on to the arrow.

The balance point of an arrow has caused considerable discussion in the past, but today the argument has pretty much gone by the board. At one time archers weighted the front end to bring the balance point forward, under the assumption that this would cause straighter shots. It doesn't work. A heavy arrow end provides too much total inertia, causing undue buckling at the loose, leading to erratic flight, warpage and possible breakage. And with the center of gravity at the front, the arrow in flight tends to act something like a weather vane, yawing slightly upwind. This slightly sidewise flight path increases air resistance, decreases flight time, and necessitates a high trajectory. Under heavy wind conditions, it can break the arrow on impact. The commonly accepted balance point today is about 1¾ inches front of center.

Torque is one area of bow design with which manufacturers are still hotly experimenting. This is the tendency of a bow either to tilt forward and back or to twist in the hand as the arrow is loosed. It results largely from the arrow rest being to the left of center, and the drawn string's V below the nock—under the middle draw finger—rather than centered behind it. A popular torque stabilization method is simply to add weight to the bow. This increases the mass moment of inertia or general resistance to the kick or jar all bows exhibit to one degree or another.

Most companies claim they have stabilization weights built into their bows, principally concentrated in two points equidistant from the arrow rest. Some manufacturers (Bear, Colt, Wing, Howatt, for example) produce bows with obvious heavy wood projections on the handle risers, while Birnie Bows makes a few Oscillation Damper models which have attached to their fronts what look like mirror images.

The most radical design for stabilization is that pioneered by Hoyt Archery Company for its Pro Medalist series. It

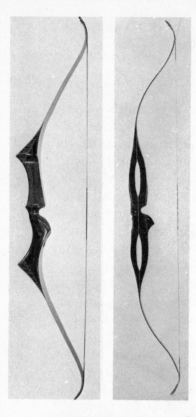

Three methods of achieving bow stabilization. Left: Bear bow, the Tamerlane ($125) features built-in stabilizers (the heavy projections). Center: Birnie Bows' Royal Caledonian ($125) employs "oscillation dampers." Right: Wing claims that its adjustable-weight Accra-Lizer ($30) can be installed on any bow to damp vibrations and torque.

incorporates two weights that look like elongated doorknobs, inch-thick metal marbles squatting on 2 to 5-inch pedestals. Another company—Herter's Inc., Weseca, Minn., sporting-goods mail-order house—manufactures stabilizers attachable to nearly any bow. The company claims that its devices can increase scores up to 30 percent, and that chronograph tests show that stabilizers affect cast at a rate of less than 2 feet per second. Herter's units come in six different weights and lengths, the longest jutting out from the bow more than a half foot.

We've come a long way in bow design in the last decade or two. But though recent advances have been truly amazing, chances are that in the next few years even more startling materials and designs will be developed, and archery tackle will approach even more closely the elusive ideal.

Chapter 12

TACKLE CARE AND REPAIR

W HEN the old bowman and the young bowman returned from the day's hunt, the young man told a tale of abject woe while the old bowhunter cleaned his pheasants. The young bowman had flushed a dozen birds, but failed to hit one. He spotted a squirrel, but succeeded only in frightening it as his arrow lodged high in an oak. Then late in the day, on the way back to camp, he met face-to-face with a buck. But his quickly loosed arrow passed harmlessly into the brush.

"Let me take a look at those arrows of yours," said the old bowhunter, picking up the young man's shafts. One by one he examined them, separating them into four piles.

"These have crooked heads," he said, indicating one set. "Look here." He held one horizontally by the nock, resting the broadhead collar upon his upraised left thumb and forefinger, and spun the arrow as he sighted down it. "See how the point makes a little circle?"

He picked up an arrow from another pile. "Your fletching needs help here," he said. "No way in the world for these to go straight." One feather was coming loose at the front, battered from sliding along the ground. Another was matted from slithering under wet leaves. The old bowhunter picked up the third arrow from the pile. "You re-fletched this feather, didn't you?" The young bowman nodded. "The original fletching was slightly spiraled, but you cemented the loose feather on straight."

Arrows in the third group had shaft trouble. One had indentations along it from being bumped. Another had begun to split. Picking up a third, the old bowhunter held it to the light and slowly spun it as he squinted and sighted along the shaft. "This corkscrew has had it. But we'll save the feathers and head. Be able to use them later.

"These are fine," he said, pointing to the last pile. It held two arrows.

"Now let's fix them up," said the old bowhunter. With a pair of smooth-jawed pliers he carefully straightened those broadheads that were bent, sighting along and spinning the shafts till the tips pointed true. Those that were on crooked he heated with a match to loosen the cement. Then he removed the heads and with a tool like a pencil sharpener smoothed out the tapers, removing as little wood as possible. Then he dabbed a little fishing rod ferrule cement in the head holes, reglued the points, and sighted again to make sure of their straightness.

He sharpened each blade with a pocket hone, adding a drop of oil, then wiped them clean on his hunting pants and tilted each edge to catch the light reflection. "Broadheads must be razory," he commented. "Otherwise they just push arteries aside. Besides, the law requires razor-sharp blades."

One of the plastic nocks was askew, so the old bowhunter cut it off with his knife, replaced it with another from his tackle kit, cementing it on with airplane glue.

Moving to the bad-fletching pile, he reset the loose feather with a dab of fletching cement. Then carefully he sliced off the mis-set feather and, holding it tight with pins, glued it back on the original mark with a slight spiral. Into the steam from the boiling coffeepot he thrust the arrow with the matted feathers. Two feathers popped back in shape; the third failed to revive. The old bowhunter cut this off and lightly sanded away the dried cement. Then from the shaft that had begun to split he gently removed a feather. "Good thing these are from the same set," he said. "Chances are they're matched. They're from the same side of the bird, of course."

He then picked up the arrows from the shaft-trouble pile and walked over to the glowing potbelly stove. "Notice that I won't try to straighten shafts over an open flame or steam," he said. "Too much moisture can ruin these compressed cedar shafts, and flame could blister the finish." He held each warped shaft between thumbs and forefingers and bent them against the warp, then turned from the fire, holding each in this position. When they cooled, he rolled them along the flat top of the large stove grill (now cool), testing them for wobble. Each took two or three heatings before he was satisfied.

The arrow with dents presented a problem. "We'll have to be careful. Not much hope." Quickly he passed the dents over the coffeepot's escaping steam, and all but one dent filled in again. "This last dent is too deep. When you get home fill it with plastic wood and sand it smooth. It'll probably be good only for field practice, though.

"Now you've got a good set again," said the old bowhunter. But the young bowman refused to believe that arrows were his big problem. Until he thought about it the next evening as he stood at the big slab table cleaning his day's game.

As any experienced archer knows, sooner than he'd like, the pile of maimed, broken, time-worn arrows grows, and the number of still-matched missiles shrinks. But also as old archers know, it's much easier to keep arrows out of the repair heap than to fix them, and by taking care, they'll stay out that much longer.

Fletching gives the most headaches, and among freshmen archers more feathers are destroyed by withdrawing arrows backwards than by any other method. If an arrow has penetrated into a target so far that the feathers enter the face, pull it all the way through. If you're new at the game, feather toughness will surprise you—if they're pulled through *with* the grain. When an arrow has slithered under the grass up to a tree, dig around the fletching and make sure no grass roots are entangled before pulling it out.

When a feather begins to break apart, put the arrow aside for later fixing. Don't keep shooting it; you won't hit the mark anyway. Soon you'll have another fouled-up arrow from which you can cop a feather. This is one reason, by the way, for buying matched arrows by the dozen. Ordinarily you shoot six at a time; when one goes bad you can substitute another from the other six and have assurance that it matches.

Wet-weather shooting presents special problems for feathers. Here's a hint: Carry a plastic bag with you to be slipped over your quiver in case of a storm. When wet weather is expected, some bowhunters spray the feathers with waterproofing oil, the solution fishermen use to waterproof floating dry flies. Others simply give them a light rub with liquid car wax.

When replacing feathers on new glass or aluminum shafts, wash the shafts with detergent the first time; from then on just sand lightly and follow directions on the tube of cement.

Incorrect storage can take the life out of feathers. If left in the quiver, for example, they'll be pressed out of shape. If you haven't an arrow-storer, keep your missiles in the original carton or use a corrugated cardboard box with holes punched through one side. Clips screwed to the wall also are good, as are two layers of heavy hardware cloth. Toss a few mothballs into the box to keep vermin out of the feathers, and keep the box in a cool, relatively dry place. Kept through the winter in a steam-heated house, arrows might contract so much the piles will come off. To correct, stand them overnight, pile down in a quarter-filled glass of water before using

Arrows broken off at the pile can be refitted, but should be given to someone who has a shorter draw. An arrow a half inch shorter than you're used to means a possible over-draw, and if not drawn to anchor, it will have lower trajec-tory, erratic flight.

An arrow split or cracked near the nock should be thrown away. One cracked near the point may be salvaged for prac-tice shooting in areas where loss is probable. Bend the shaft to open the break wide, squeeze in waterproof glue, wrap a piece of wax paper around the break area, and bind tightly with tape until dry.

Check occasionally to see that your arrows are grouping; record hits of a few ends by arrow number. For a quick check, have someone stand behind you to watch the missiles as they leave the bow. Best seeing is against the light—into the setting sun, for instance. If the arrows fishtail—bobble around before straightening out—something is on crooked, or the shaft is warped. If the tails kick down as the arrows leave the bow, you may be nocking too low; if they take off tail high, try nocking lower.

As though you haven't enough to worry about already, here's a batch of arrow DON'TS to keep in mind:

. . . Don't shoot bent aluminum arrows. If they're not too bad you can straighten them with an arrow-straightening rig. Manufacturers will straighten not badly bent aluminum arrows for about fifty cents each.

. . . Don't shoot broadheads into anything except game; they'll lose their edge, break off, bang out of shape. Use blunt-headed piles of broadhead weight for practice. Don't shoot at nonpenetrable targets at all.

. . . Don't store broadheads where they can rub together. Don't store wood arrows for protracted times at an angle, nor lay them on a shelf, nor in a quiver with the fletching bunched together.

. . . Don't shoot arrows that have something wrong with them. A slightly bent arrow can be fixed easily; a slightly

An arrow box of some sort for storage and carrying is desirable. This one, designed for 36 arrows, is of ¾-inch plywood with hinged lid and front of ¼-inch plywood.

bent arrow that has been shot one more time may be irreparable.

. . . Don't buy arrows singly or at cut-rate prices; save up until you can get a matched dozen. A single mis-spined arrow can throw off a whole round.

. . . Don't pull arrows from targets by the nocks. Too easily bent that way. Hold them near the target with one hand while you push against the face with the other. Carry them by the points so the feathers will spread apart.

. . . Don't shoot more than a dozen arrows per end at a close target. They'll hit each other more often than you think.

. . . Don't wax your target arrows; makes pulling them from butts too difficult.

. . . Don't lean your target against a stone wall.

Bow care is much less complicated. Mostly it's just common sense: don't leave the bow in a tense position; don't twist the arms or bend them unevenly; keep from extremes in temperature and humidity.

Never, for example, leave your bow in a tightly closed car or car trunk in the heat of summer; the air temperature inside can reach 125° or more—too high for man or bow. Crack your windows a bit and open the air vents. Similarly, don't leave your bow lying in the hot sun; keep it as comfortable as you yourself. And if it does get hot, wait until it cools before stringing. "A bow should never be used, or even strung, when heat inside the bow is higher than atmospheric temperature," says a spokesman from Colt Fire Arms, maker of bows. If left in the sun while strung, the weight of a bow might drop dramatically. Incidentally, Colt says that most of the bows returned for repair met their ends by being slammed under auto trunk lids.

In winter, bows should be flexed every so often to keep them limber.

Ski-Doo courtesy Elliott & Hutchins, Malone, New York

Cold weather brings problems, too, particularly with heavy hunting bows. If your bow is cold, flex it a few times before pulling to a full draw. Otherwise you might be left with little more than a handle. Be especially careful if it seems to bind, if it doesn't pull as smoothly as usual. In fact, leave your good bow at home in subfreezing weather, if practical. If not, flex it every so often on those cold fall hunts. Keeps you warm, too.

Gradual flexing also breaks in new bows, and it's a good idea too for bows that haven't been used in some time. Reason: a back subjected to drying is likely to have lost part of its tensile strength. If you find an ancient bow in finish, wet the back with water and when it has dried, soak it well with oil. Lemon oil is good. Break it in gradually, then refinish it.

Protect the finish of your bow with an occasional polishing of paste-type furniture wax. Keeps moisture balanced, too. Wax on leather parts takes a while to work in, but it the attic, better not draw it at all. Instead, scrape off the does a good job of protection. When hunting, protect it even more by using what is called a sock (also a *sox*), a tubular piece of cloth, often wool jersey, which snugs around the limbs. A sock also cuts down on reflected sunlight.

Some bowmen use tape to cut sun reflection, for camouflage, and for attaching such things as sights and bow quivers. This is all right if you give the bow a good coating of wax polish before, and remove the tape immediately after; manufacturers often refuse to honor their guarantees if encrusted tape has spoiled a bow's finish. For camouflaging, the best idea is to use camouflage wax that can be wiped off, available in stick form.

A bow's arrow rest gets the most wear. Fortunately, it's easily replaced. Just cut off the old and glue on the new (fashioned yourself or store-bought) with waterproof cement. After replacing the rest, check carefully to see if you need to change your nocking point.

Nicks—even small ones—are rough on bows, so take care not to drop yours or bang it against rocks. A nick along the back edge of a fiberglass bow can cause slivering and eventual breakage. Small nicks can be removed by sanding, but should a large one occur, send the bow back to the manufacturer for filling in. If your deeply nicked bow is a wooden one, the only hope may be to have the whole thing scraped and worked down to a lighter weight. One danger signal is when a bow starts to pull easily; that may mean the start of a fracture. Watch out.

Dry-drawing—pulling the string all the way back without

an arrow—is dangerous for a few reasons. You may overdraw. You may grasp the string at the wrong place and pull one limb more than the other and cause a strain. And you might slip and let the string fly forward—always a bad policy, because dry-firing puts an immense strain on both the bow and the string. If the string breaks, the limbs might fly forward with such force they break. Surprisingly, the inertia of an arrow is enough to hold things back.

When you're through shooting, unstring the bow so that the tension over a period won't weaken it. Some archers unstring their bows half a dozen times a day. They needn't. It's enough if bows are unstrung every evening.

A good storage method is to place the bow horizontally on two pegs that fit the recurves. Don't lean your weapon in the corner; over a protracted period the weight tends to weaken the lower limb—particularly older-type bows. The best place is right up on your wall (but not against the chimney) where the air can circulate and where everyone can see it. Don't put it in the attic (too hot) or basement (too damp) or garage (too cold). If you buy your bow from a local distributor rather than directly from the manufacturer, make sure you don't get the one displayed in his front windows; hot sun shining through a storefront can ruin the best of bows.

Above all, don't overdraw. "A bow fully drawn is a bow seven-eighths broken," the old archery saying goes. Don't pass that other eighth. Keep your tall friends away from your bow.

If you notice that your bow tips are misaligned ("twisted limbs"), the cause probably was incorrect stringing or storage or the buildup of internal pressurage through aging. Recommended procedure is to find a professional bowyer to fix it up, but if none is around and you're in a hurry, here's a tip from Hoyt Archery Co.: "All that is needed is an electric hot plate and about five minutes of time. Heat the base of the recurve 5 to 12 inches from the tip. Hold approximately 6 inches above the plate and heat only the flat surfaces of the back and face until they are warm or slightly hot to the touch. *Do not overheat or scorch the finish.* Now, with one hand on the tip and the other grasping the mid limb, twist the tip end in the opposite direction to which it has gone out of alignment. Hold in this position for 10 to 20 seconds and then permit to cool to air temperature. . . . To check alignment, brace bow and observe how the bowstring lifts from and settles back into the grooves of the recurve." One or two such treatments are usually enough. If not, return the bow to the factory.

Strings can cause all sorts of trouble, particularly when they clandestinely part company under the nocking point, a favorite place because of the constant sharp-angle flexing. If you notice your serving bunching or bumping, snip it loose and see what's going on under there. If your string is starting to break, dump it. Strings are cheap, bows are not. If the bumping was your imagination, or if the serving had started to fray from wear, replace the windings. Use any heavy, soft-finish thread (large archery stores sell serving thread cheaply), and when you wind it, firm the coils together, but don't wind too tightly. A too-tight length of serving will help wear out the string rather than protect it. Watch the end loops, too. If your bow nocks are the least bit rough your string is likely to let loose here.

Rub bowstrings every so often with paraffin or beeswax to make them waterproof and help hold the strands together. Some bowmen switch their strings end-for-end at what they guess is the half-life mark. This changes the nocking point a couple of inches and makes the string last a little longer.

Target matts have a way of standing up well, then suddenly going to pieces. The cause often is that they have been allowed to dry out and become brittle. An occasional sprinkling with plain water will help here. On the other hand, matts and butts shouldn't be rained on, or mildew will set in, as well as a variety of flourishing insect life. Saunders Archery Target Co. says its matts should have 15 percent moisture content, but usually arrive with only about 9 percent. Therefore 6 percent water (by weight) should be added.

If it's awkward to take your targets in at night, keep old tarps or plastic tablecloths over them. When you do take in a target, don't roll it; that will soften even the most tightly packed matts. In the field, you may have trouble with rats, mice, and an occasional cow.

When the target matts finally start to go, tightening the cords helps to delay the process. Just pull them out and tie the loops. A big help in extending matt life is the addition of extra backing, especially when your arrows start to sail through. One cheap reinforcer can be made from two strips of truck inner tube about 10 inches wide and 28 inches long. Cross the bands over the back of the matt and fasten them at the edge with spikes driven in at an angle. A better backup is another, smaller matt. A 16-inch matt costs only about one-seventh that of a 4-foot matt, but attached to the center of the back the smaller one will double the life of the large one. Another thing to keep in mind is that the use of long-nose arrow piles will greatly reduce matt wear.

Eventually, you will ruin your targets, your bow, your arrows. All of them. But by following care and repair rules, life expectancy can be dramatically increased.

Chapter 13

FIELD ARCHERY

Y OU finish with the day's work, grab your bow and and a handful of old arrows, and set off on a leisurely stroll through the woods. A distant poplar trunk catches your eye, and you loose three arrows at it, hitting dead center with the third. You pick up the grounded arrows, use pliers to pull out the third, look around for another likely target. You spot a paper scrap on a nearby knoll, and kneeling under the tree to get bow-room, you pin the paper to the hill.

Some 70 yards from the knoll a five-gallon oil can lies half buried in a sand pit. Your bow comes up arrow drawn, the string twangs, and in a high parabola the missile arcs over a thicket, lands with a distant clunk right on target. The shaft is split from pile to nock, but you don't care; with a self-satisfied nod you remind yourself that the arrow was an old one anyway.

This is elementary field archery, identical with the ancient sport of rovers in which longbow soldiers in the absence of enemies would take to the field to shoot stumps and bags of matted leaves at varying distances. Based on the hunt, field archery teaches you to be flexible, to hone your judgment of distance, to be able to adapt to strange terrain, to varied weather, and evergreen branches grabbing with malice.

Field archery started centuries ago. But when gunpowder changed warfare from something like a rough-and-ready

154

sport to more like a business, and when rifles replaced bows for hunting, archery became civilized, moved from the woods to creeping-bent lawns. Field archery hung on only among the unsophisticated—the backwoods hillbilly too poor to afford shells or the farm boy, fashioning his bow from straight-grained hickory.

Target archery became the sport of ladies and gentlemen. No longer was it important to make that first shot count. With target archery the first shot—or first dozen—really didn't matter much, for by the time totals were marked, dozens of arrows had been fired.

Along came someone who learned to use a leaf or twig lying on the ground as a sighting aid, then decided to substitute a white ball. Because nothing in the rules made the innovation illegal, the point-of-aim marker was subsequently adopted universally, and "instinctive" shooting almost joined the dodo for all it was used. Though an instinctive shooter may beat out the point-of-aimer in the first half-dozen shots, as soon as the POA man gets centered in he leaves the opposition back on the trail.

Then in the 1930's an interesting new sport began to grow in America: bowhunting. But archers who had developed proficiency on the target range—shooting innumerable arrows at predetermined and very familiar distances—out in the wild were flops. By the time they had picked their POA or judged the distance and adjusted their bow sights, whatever they were after had moved to the next township.

Some of these men—notably the Redland, California, founders of the National Field Archery Association (NFAA) —became disgusted with formalized, almost ritualistic target archery. They decided that perhaps the old bare-bow method of shooting had something to it after all, and forgot all about POA, sights, and tape-measured distances.

With just a touch of egotism, they called their new/old technique "instinctive," and it wasn't long before they began to bring home the bacon—or at least an occasional rabbit.

Problem was, however, that they couldn't get enough practice in the hunting season. What was needed was a regular series of targets—substitutes for game—laid over a course which boasted a whole forestland of hunting-type situations. The men banded together in a loose-knit organization to work out the details, and in 1934, to build the first field course. Says John L. Yount, one of the founders: "This was a club of target archers, not by choice but by necessity. There simply was no other kind of archery. But the members of this club just were not target archers at heart." They actually were field archers, but the term had no clear meaning until 1939, the year this group of hunting-oriented archers founded the NFAA.

Talk about field archery and you talk about hunting— whether or not you ever expect to go after anything alive. However, there has been a subtle shift in emphasis in the last few years: more and more people are seen on field courses who not only are disinterested in hunting, but are almost antagonistic to it. "We have a large group in NFAA who are tournament archers," says George E. Rohrbach, Acting Secretary. "And as such, field archery to them is merely a variety of target archery."

Nevertheless, field work is based on the hunt; target archery is not. And because of this, there is a basic difference between the two. The object is the same—hitting the target; it's just a matter of technique, with a few rules tossed in, that makes the difference. Just how target and field archery differ is apparent with a close look at the steps of the shooting cycle:

THE STANCE, when the field shooter is working open territory, differs little from the conventional, though the feet might be spread a bit more to brace against uneven ground or wind. Flexibility, however, is the rule of field work, so you'll have to assume some stances that on the target field would be ludicrous. Sometimes the only way you can see your quarry is to kneel, for example. (One method: right knee on the ground, left knee upright, bow slanted to the left of the upright knee.) Or you may have to get down on both knees, in which case you'll have to work out your own bow position —just so long as you remain relaxed and don't screw into a position where you lack sufficient freedom to adjust.

NOCKING in field work is identical with that of target archery. Only difference is that you'll often nock minutes—occasionally hours—before drawing. One other variance: The target archer usually looks to see what he's doing; the hunter does not. He keeps his eye on the target and nocks by feel—the reason for that little ridge on the arrow nock parallel with the cock feather.

DRAWING differs mainly in the anchor point. It's high in order to bring the arrow closer to the eye, and the head is tilted slightly to the right to bring the eye closer to the string. The bow, too, is canted, about 25 degrees. If it weren't, the string would be in the line of vision, and the upper bow limb might be distracting. Also, a slanted bow cuts down on overhead foliage problems. When kneeling, of course, you have no choice if your bow size is conventional.

AIMING was covered in Chapter 9, but these points deserve re-emphasis: 1) Concentrate on the target, not the pile. 2) Estimate distances subconsciously, rather than in measured units (yards, feet). 3) Keep both eyes open to take advantage of your binocular vision. 4) Draw fully, even if the quarry is only ten feet away.

No "artificial" aiming devices are allowed. Under NFAA rules archers shooting in the instinctive class are forbidden to use "any sights, marks, or blemishes that could be used in aiming," including even a pencil mark on the string.

HOLDING is a question much discussed. Some field men figure it's better to get off two or three shots while the chance is there. Most successful bowhunters, however, hold and

Enlargements from 35-mm sequence camera show Fred Bear in action on the Alaskan Peninsula in May, 1962. Fred and his guide, Ed Bilderback, are hidden behind a rock as a bear approaches.

Bear continues along beach. Arrow is nocked in the 65-lb. Kodiak bow, ready for drawing.

Bear senses something, stops to look over hunters.

He decides that they are part of the scenery and continues on. Fred, bow at full draw, waits until bear's front leg is fully forward.

Arrow has struck, burying itself to the feathers behind front leg. Bear roars, runs towards the photographer who abandoned his job . . .

. . . until the bear passes him, when composure allows him to continue the sequence. Shortly afterward, the bear dropped dead.

Fred poses with bear. It weighed 810 pounds.

Photos, Courtesy Bear Archery Company

sight for at least a full second, enough to feel really "set," and to adjust if the set feeling is missing.

RELEASING is identical with that done on the target range— smooth, easy, pluckless. Just let the string slither off your glove tips as though equipped with greasy ball bearings.

FOLLOW-THROUGH is another area of contention. But bow-hunters who return to camp with game rather than stories make it a practice to hold everything a bit after loosing the arrow, making sure they don't relax prematurely.

Equipment for field shooting differs only in part from that of target work. Short bows are preferred in wooded areas; lugging a branch-tangling longbow along gets downright exasperating.

A somewhat heavier-than-normal bow also is required in the field, one that will give a relatively flat trajectory and is strong enough to kill rather than wound. Many state laws, in fact, specify a minimum poundage for hunting bows. It's interesting, however, that statistics gathered in a recent year indicated that 42.1 percent of deer kills made with bows pulling 50 to 60 pounds showed complete penetration, while only 16.6 percent of those downed by bows drawing more than 60 pounds showed complete penetration. Reason: in the excitement of the hunt, big bows just aren't pulled to full draw. In field tournaments, official rules allow any bow except the crossbow.

Because the whole purpose in field work is simulation of the hunt, field arrows differ somewhat from those used for target practice. Standard target arrows can be used, but the potential deerslayer who practices with them all summer, becoming quite proficient, will be chagrined when the big moment presents itself and the hunting arrow skittles along at the hooves. The source of his trouble: broadheads, being heavier, are slower moving, drop more quickly. The potential hunter, practicing on the field range, therefore should use blunt or pointed roving arrows as closely matched in weight to broadheads as possible. Also, target arrows are too light to stand up under rough field use; a beautifully fashioned $18-a-dozen set will be transformed to a bent and twisted pile of curios after a heavy field session of glancing off trees and rocks.

The real thing—broadheads—should not be used, however; they'll not only rip apart targets, but will imbed themselves so deeply in wood that most of the time they are destroyed. The fact is, no matter what kind of arrow you use, you'll run through more in a single season of field work than in a whole decade on the target range.

Target faces in the field differ considerably from those used in target archery. The big thing in conventional target shooting is conformity—identical targets placed exact distances from the shooter. The opposite is true in field work: the distances are usually unknown, and target faces come in strange sizes:

24-in. face with 12-in. center and 4-in. aiming spot
18-in. face with 9-in. center and 3-in. aiming spot
12-in. face with 6-in. center and 2-in. aiming spot
6-in. face with 3-in. center and 1-in. aiming spot

Rather than colored, these targets ordinarily are black and white—the spots and outer rim black and the middle ring white. When animal targets are used—often beautiful prints of natural-color paintings—the black and white rings are eliminated except for outlines, with the center spots of a contrasting color.

For striking inside the center ring (the spot, or "pimple," is for aiming convenience only) the shooter gets 5 points; for the outer circle, 3. As in target archery, an arrow sticking between the rings counts for the higher rating, so long as the ring line itself cannot be seen. Skids or bounces into the target don't count, but arrows bouncing off the target or passing through count 3 each.

In addition, the NFAA in 1961 made official the Hunter's Round, in which all-black targets with white aiming spots are used. These vary from 6 to 24 inches and distances run from 11 to 70 yards. Another new sequence is the Animal Round, in which archers shoot at various animal targets. In this, the high-score center is oblong, while also-ran scores result from hits between the center and the animal's outline. Each archer shoots only until he makes a hit, with a maximum of three arrows, none of which is shot from the same distance stake. Scoring is 16 or 20 for the first arrow (depending on whether the center or secondary scoring area is hit), 10 or 14 for the second, 4 or 8 for the third. Bull's-eye sizes vary between 9 x 14 inches (black bear) to 3⅝ by 2¼ inches (turtle). Incidentally, all NFAA authorized target faces carry the association's emblem in the center no matter who the manufacturer.

In a regulation field tournament shoot, some interesting rules go into effect, not all of which are ordinarily followed. They include:

. . . No practicing on the course allowed the same day. The targets are sneakily changed around by the officials so archers on the home team won't have an unfair advantage, and so that no below-board archer can beforehand pace off the distances.

. . . If any regulation *target archery* matts are used, the center of the face should be moved at least 8 vertical inches from the matt center. If more than one such matt is used in sequence, the faces should vary at least 16 inches in consecutive shots, and on every third one, the edge of the target face must come to within 3 inches of the ground. Throws off even the best target men with range-finder vision.

. . . If you're a woman, you can shoot against the men, but

if you are a man, you must stick with your own kind—no shooting in women's events.

. . . Not only is the use of field glasses disallowed, but you can't even consult notes that might help you get a higher score.

Sighting rules, however, apply only to "instinctive" tournaments, contests in which only bare-bow shooters compete. There are also "free style" field tournaments, in which any kind of sight is okay so long as it isn't calibrated for that specific course. The reason that the NFAA decided to let in the deviators is that the organization found a whole batch of men who couldn't stand the dullness of conventional target archery, yet didn't quite go along with the informality of instinctive shooting. They wanted to use sights. Some of these were hunters, and accounted for a nice percentage of game each year—so they really belonged in the field archery group. To satisfy everyone, the NFAA decided to hold *two* annual championship matches concurrently. The bare-bow men now vie for the honor of being National Field Champion, while sight users try out for National Free Style Field Champion. Bare-bow shooters and free-style men never officially compete against each other, for it has been proven that on field ranges the men with sights walk all over instinctive archers. (Better not mention that to a bare-bow man, though.)

When once you've experienced field archery—even if it means simply a few roving walks through the woods popping off at whatever strikes your fancy—you're either hooked or you'll remain satisfied with the target range. If you become addicted, you'll not be satisfied until you join a club. None around? Maybe not, but you may be surprised. Ask your local archery-tackle distributor. If he doesn't know, get in touch with the National Field Archery Association (Route 2, Box 514, Redlands, California) to find the nearest club. If there really aren't any close, you might consider founding your own.

Forming the club

There's a quiverful of advantages to being a club member: companionship with others with similar interests; constant exchanges of information on new equipment, points of technique, used-tackle availability; a place to get way from it all; and of course, the range—really, the whole purpose of a field club, and as important to the field archer as a golf course is to a golfer.

If you are thinking of chartering a club, gather together a few local archers and toss around some ideas on possible grounds to use for the range, for this is the first order of business for any prospective club. Ideally, one of your members may have land of his own that for a minimal fee he will rent to the club. Another prospective land lender might be the local rod and gun club; archery is being looked upon with more favor nowadays, and the local club might go along with your ideas. The city park authority might have land that you can use (you may even get free park department maintenance), even though you may have to throw it open to the public. Or the local school may have an archery program of its own with which you could affiliate—in exchange for the use of school property. In addition, many tracts are just lying fallow—the owner lives in another part of the country, he's holding land until the value rises or he owns a few acres just to have it. Some of these absentee landowners may give you permission to use their acreage just so they can feel it's being used. Or if you don't mind more work, you may find a piece of inaccessible woodland that you can use in return for making a road into it. Be sure, however, to give the owner *some* rent money (say, $5 a year), and get him to sign a long-term lease. Otherwise, when he sees how nicely you've fixed up the place he may want to move in.

A good size for a range is about 10 acres for fourteen targets, twice that for a full twenty-eight target course. And the best site is rolling woodland; varied elevations make for

interesting archery, and the overhead canopy of trees cuts
way down on underbrush.

With land possibilities extant, you probably will have little
difficulty getting the core of a club solidified. Work out some
sort of a yearly budget, including such expenses as land
rental, butt costs, storage space rental or cost of materials
to build a clubhouse (save labor costs by doing the work
yourself), miscellaneous expenses for regional and national
affiliation, correspondence, etc. With these in mind, make a
conservative estimate of possible club membership, and decide on dues. Too-high dues mean fewer members, while
dues at too low a figure mean financial trouble.

With details worked out in a general sort of way, assume
the temporary presidency and call a mass meeting. If enough
potential members show up (if they don't, don't be discour-
aged; as the club gets rolling, the membership should soar),
vote on adoption of a constitution and bylaws, including
such things as fees and dues. (A sample constitution, suggested by NFAA, is presented in the Appendix.) Then at
that meeting, or the next, elect officers. Your club is off and
rolling.

Later, you'll want to affiliate with NFAA, then with nearby
clubs, forming a league—otherwise your shoot dates may
conflict. Clubs can band together and sponsor regional
shoots. Affiliation with the state organization is beneficial;
many such associations represent archery interests in the
state legislature, deal with the game commission, schedule
state tournaments and act as clearinghouses for news.

Other items your club might keep in mind:

. . . Give junior members a voice. Not only are they your
future backbone, but with responsibility, all that wild energy
can be put to use—maintaining the range, for example.

. . . Try to arrange for *something* to happen almost every
week.

. . . It's tough work, but a periodic bulletin of scores, gossip
and tackle information is a big solidifier for a club. In the

absence of this, post current scores in a glass-fronted water-proof display box or in the window of the local sports store.

. . . Charge target fees for all tournaments, enough so there is a little left over. Don't, however, overcharge for regional tournaments. If you do, other groups will soon fail to send representatives.

. . . Frown on overlapping memberships—topflight archers who belong to half a dozen clubs for the sole purpose of stocking up on prizes.

. . . Your secretary is the second most important person in the club—maybe most important. If he (or she) isn't much of an archer, so what? The technique of addition is occasionally as important as the ability to pick off a buck at 40 yards.

. . . Keep in close touch with the local school physical-education instructors, your nearby dealers, and perhaps a local official or two. Politic.

. . . Last, a thought from target maker Saunders Co.: A course is a place to have archery fun, to improve ability and to hold tournaments—in that order. Don't get in the tournament rut. Foursome-type shooting, handicap systems and novelty shoots are the lifeblood of any club.

Building the range

A good range is one that presents a variety of problems, where the unexpected is the mode, the distances never quite the same, the lay of the land or arrangement of hazards always a bit surprising. If your land is in the rolling Poconos, your range will be interesting no matter how you work it. But a rugged landscape isn't essential for an exciting range; any area can be interesting if the designers take their time to plan it in detail first. If they don't, chances are the range will quickly seem dull and loss of membership will result.

When you start planning, keep in mind the advantages of parking space, eventual building site, picnic area (for non-shooting family members), drinking water and electricity.

But first, get at least a few targets up, and get your club roving. The clubhouse, moving targets, and NFAA approval can come later. Put out temporary targets along open spaces in a giant golf-course-like ellipse—a flour sack full of dirt, a cardboard box of leaves and sod, a few balloons, a figure cut from wood, a gunnysack stuffed with bags, a sod bank or a pile of sand.

You start at No. 1, shoot till you hit each target, and he who gets around with the least number of shots wins. Or the "Eastern" method of scoring may be best for you. Each archer shoots until he hits the target, with a maximum of four arrows. He scores one point for his first shot, two for his second, etc., and stops when he hits. A strikeless end counts five. Low man wins.

Along with getting temporary targets up and in use, send for the NFAA Official Handbook. Costs $2 and gives excellent step-by-step instructions for making a field course, as well as a batch of other useful information. It belongs on the bookshelf of every serious archer.

Now to the planning. If you have available only 10 acres or less, make a single 14-target course with two carefully thought-out shooting positions for each target, so designed that the shooters go around the loop first in one direction, again in another. Pay particular attention to safety; you'll probably have to do some fancy juggling, but make it impossible for a shooter to cross between another man and his target.

With the space, you can plan a 28-target course in two giant loops, something like a drunken figure eight, with the clubhouse eventually located at the center. When the archer has completed one course lap, he can stop off at the clubhouse for a half-time break. Furthermore, on crowded days some groups can start at target No. 15. Also, if you have time enough for only 14 targets, the end of your shoot will put you back at the clubhouse without necessitating a long walk.

During this initial stage it's a good idea to seek the help of an experienced course-maker—someone who was in on the ground floor of building his own unit, and who can tell you the mistakes *he* made. Even better, talk your state NFAA representative into visiting your site. His opinions will be invaluable, particularly because he will be keeping in mind the standards established by the NFAA which must be met if your course is to get official sanction—something for which to aim.

Out in the woods, your first job is to walk. Take along a tablet and try to make a map of the area, including hills, land features, prominent trees, streams, possible shooting sites.

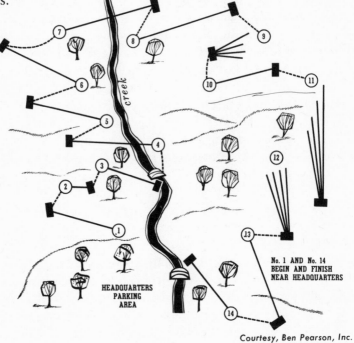

Courtesy, Ben Pearson, Inc.

Typical 14-target field range. Circled numbers indicate shooting positions; black rectangles show targets. Dotted lines are walkways between targets; straight black lines, arrow paths.

Back home, rough up a plan for half the course (14 targets), and get that settled before tackling the other half. (You've already got four approximate site locations, of course: Nos. 1, 14, 15, and 28—those in immediate proximity to your future clubhouse.) Your final scheme undoubtedly will be far different from your first map-rough, but a good couple of hours' work at home will save much energy in the field.

Use the following NFAA table as a guide for each 14-shot loop:

DISTANCE	ARROWS	FACE
15 yds.	4	12″
20 "	4	12″
25 "	4	12″
30 "	4	12″
40 "	4	18″
45 "	4	18″
50 "	4	18″
55 "	4	24″
60 "	4	24″
65 "	4	24″
35 "	4, but each from a different shooting position	18″
45, 40, 35, & 30 yds.	1 arrow at each distance	18″
80, 70, 60, & 50 "	1 arrow at each distance	24″
35, 30, 25, & 20 ft.	1 arrow at each distance	6″

These needn't—in fact, shouldn't—be in the above order, but ought to be well mixed, according to your terrain. If your range has physical limitations which make the last three items in the list (called "walk-ups" in field archery parlance) difficult to achieve, you can shoot at more than one target— say, two shots at a target low on a hill, two more at one higher up, while standing at two shooting positions.

When ready to lay things out on the field, take along a batch of rags of two different colors—one to mark probable shooting stakes, the other for the targets. Plan on using up at least a couple of days (probably more) on this step.

About to begin construction, you'll need pruning shears for snipping slapping branches, an ax or hatchet to remove trees, a mattock or grub hoe to clear out stumps and roots.

Shooting pegs should be painted white with the shot number in black. For walk-up shots, print the order number below the peg number. Distances are not marked on stakes. (Check Chapter 6 for data on targets and butts.)

For the first few weeks of your new course, ask members to carry pruning shears along with them. That way annoying overhanging branches and underbrush will be cleared with little concentrated work. It's a good idea to have a standing gentlemen's rule that all travel be done on the trails; paths will quickly be etched in permanently that way with little danger of anyone later getting lost, and the surrounding naturalness will remain unmarred. Try to hide your trail (and still keep it easy to follow) so the scenery isn't spoiled. Make it winding, a pleasant walk whether or not you're shooting.

A few more things to keep in mind:

. . . Make your trails easy to follow and pleasant on the feet. Eliminate slopes upon which a mountain goat would have troubles; you'll not want your course limited to ex-lumberjacks. If you're not married now you eventually will be, and if you can get your wife interested in hiking with you, she'll not wail about being an archery widow.

. . . Keep the shooting line about 10 feet long.

. . . Stacks of bales behind butts will cut depression caused by lost and broken arrows. Remove all trees and rocks from the immediate target vicinity for the same reason. Lost arrows mean slower games.

. . . Something really appreciated: Tie a can of insect repellant to the back of every few targets.

. . . Shots up steep hills make arrow-fetching rough. Targets on slight slopes are more deceptive anyway, for the shooter is more aware of high-angle trajectories. Shots where the foreground is hidden are especially good, because the range is not so easily guessed.

. . . Finally, make it safe. Think of stray arrows, shooting positions close to targets, ricochets, hilltop targets. No trail should cross close to a target, particularly near the rear. Forty feet is a good minimum.

To get your course approved by the NFAA (and it must be approved before official tournaments can be held there), the club secretary should contact the representative for your state, who will arrange for inspection. An approval certificate is good for two years, unless you change the course in the meantime. In case a representative is unable to inspect your course, your club can get approval by submitting affidavits to the NFAA secretary, along with explanatory maps and photos.

Chapter 14

TOURNAMENTS

THE first time you participate in a tournament, it's rough. Even if you've shot informally with all the other archers, when finally you lay your skill on the line for all to see, it shakes you.

You'll have troubles, that first time. You'll be astonished at how badly you do. Your score will be nowhere near what it is in practice. But look about you. The others are also having problems. And this holds true whether the tournament is of local target archers, national field experts, or international champions.

Contests and tournaments are held on all levels—club, area, state, national, and international—and can be broken down into about six different kinds: target, international target, field, professional, indoor and mail. Rules for each are often fluid, so to get updated versions of details, write to the appropriate authority for current regulation booklets. (Addresses are listed under "Associations" in the Appendix to this book.)

Here are tournament highlights of the various archery branches:

TARGET

In target archery tournaments, participants shoot a certain number of *ends* to make a game, or *round*. The word "end" comes from Old England. Archers would shoot toward one end of a field, then turn around and shoot toward similar targets at the other end. Spectators in the U.S., however, occasionally substituted themselves for targets, so officials long ago decided to put targets at only one end of the field and keep onlookers behind the shooters. A *perfect end* means all six arrows in the gold, something that is quite rare—so rare that if it happens in an official tournament the shooter gets a *six-golds* pin from the NAA.

A certain number of ends at different distances make up a *round*. For example, an American Round (probably the most popular in the U.S.) consists of 90 arrows shot at 60, 50, and 40 yards; i.e., five ends (30 arrows) shot at each distance. Boys and girls fifteen to eighteen years old, in addition to men and women, compete in the American Round.

In a *double American*, not surprisingly, you do it twice. Other official NAA rounds are as follows:

The York Round for men.

> 12 ends (72 arrows) at 100 yards
> 8 ends (48 arrows) at 80 yards
> 4 ends (24 arrows) at 60 yards
> > . . . for a total of 144 arrows

The National Round for women and intermediate girls (those between 15 and 18 years of age). This often is shot while the men are getting through their York round.

> 8 ends at 60 yards
> 4 ends at 50 yards
> > . . . totaling 72 arrows

The Columbia Round, designed for women, intermediate girls and junior girls (from 12 to 15).

> 4 ends at 50 yards
> 4 ends at 40 yards
> 4 ends at 30 yards
> > . . . for a total of 72 arrows

The Hereford Round, for women and intermediate boys.

> 12 ends at 80 yards
> 8 ends at 60 yards
> 4 ends at 50 yards
> > . . . for a total of 144 (same as the York).

The Junior American Round, for boys and girls 12 to 15 years.

> 5 ends at 50 yards
> 5 ends at 40 yards
> 5 ends at 30 yards
> > . . . for a total of 90 (same as the American).

The Junior Columbia Round, for those under 12.

> 4 ends at 40 yards
> 4 ends at 30 yards
> 4 ends at 20 yards
> > . . . for a total of 72 arrows.

The Team Rounds

Men and Intermediate Boys: 16 ends (96 arrows) at 60 yards.
Women and Intermediate Girls: 16 ends at 50 yards.
Junior Boys and Girls (from 12 to 15): 16 ends at 40 yards.
Cadet Boys (to 12 years): 16 ends at 30 yards.
Cadet Girls: 16 ends at 20 yards.

The NAA has evolved a classification system based on scores shot during special double American Rounds held by individual clubs or larger organizations, and registered in advance for the purpose. Ratings are entered on the backs of archers' NAA membership cards, and a classification is mandatory if an individual is to shoot in an official NAA tournament.

Classification is based on the following scores:

Sunday afternoon means tournaments all across the country. Here the New Jersey Archery Association meets in Willowbrook Park on New York's Staten Island.

Class	Men	Women
AA	1,400 and up (out of 1,620)	1,300 and up
A	1,250 to 1,399	1,150 to 1,299
B	1,000 to 1,249	950 to 1,149
C	Below 1,000	Below 950

(Most NAA archers are in the A and B classes)

In target archery scoring, the highest arrow value is listed first. That is, if the arrows as shot are 7, 5, 5, 9, 0, 1, they would be listed on the score card as 9, 7, 5, 5, 1, 0, (or X, for

Scene from the 1963 National Wheelchair Games, an annual event sponsored by the Bulova School of Watchmaking. Winners qualify for the U.S. Team and shoot in international wheelchair events. Americans nearly always capture top prizes.

the miss). Conventionally, an archer removes his own arrows and calls out the value to his partner, who fills in the card. In an official tournament, however, the Field Officer will appoint a Target Captain to remove arrows.

When an arrow hits between two colors, the higher value counts, so long as the arrow breaks the inside edge of the black ring-separating line. Customarily, when the Target Captain first approaches the target he examines it to see if there are any such arrows, and if so, he announces his decisions. Then if nobody objects, he pulls the questionable arrows out, sticks them in the appropriate color, then scores.

If an archer somehow grabs an extra arrow and shoots seven rather than six, he loses his most valuable hit. An arrow rebounding or passing through the target (and witnessed) counts seven points. If one sticks in the target, falls down and hangs there, the shooting is halted, the arrow picked up and stuck in solidly where its point is lodged.

INTERNATIONAL TARGET ARCHERY

In international shooting, *the* tournament is the biannual (odd-numbered years) FITA Rounds, the Federation Internationale de Tir à L'Arc, or International Federation of Target Archers. Rounds are as follows:

Men's Round: 6 ends at 90 meters (98.4 yards)
6 ends at 70 meters (76.6 yards)
6 ends at 50 meters (54.7 yards)
6 ends at 30 meters (32.8 yards)
. . . totaling 144 arrows.

Women's Round: 6 ends at 70 meters (76.6 yards)
6 ends at 60 meters (65.6 yards)
6 ends at 50 meters (54.7 yards)
6 ends at 30 meters (32.8 yards)
. . . totaling 144 arrows.

At the two longer distances in each round a standard 48-inch target is used; the 50- and 30-meter distance calls for an 80-cm (about 32-inch) face. On both targets the five rings are split in half, so instead of scoring 9-7-5-3-1, you score 10-9-8-7-6-5-4-3-2-1. Another rule somewhat odd to Americans: no magnifying or prismatic sights permitted. Before 1956, in fact, no sight at all was allowed in FITA shoots.

FIELD

Field archers shoot at various targets at diverse distances over irregular ground. An NFAA course is made up of two adjacent 14-target *units* arranged on a trail through the woods, something like a deep-forest golf course. Once around this 28-target course, or twice around a 14-target unit, makes up a round.

Four face sizes are used in the most popular form of field archery, the Field Round:

A 24-inch face with a 12-inch center bull with a 4-inch spot
An 18-inch face with a 9-inch bull and a 3-inch spot
A 12-inch face with a 3-inch bull and a 1-inch spot
A 6-inch face with a 3-inch bull and a 1-inch spot

The center black spot is for aiming; no additional points are gained by striking it. The inner white circle, including the spot, counts 5 on a regular field roving round; the outer black ring counts 3. Each archer shoots four arrows at each of the fourteen targets. Ordinarily, the shooting position stakes do not indicate the yardage to the target.

In most cases the arrows are shot from a single post (a white stake driven into the ground). Four of the targets, however, are called *walk-up*; shooting takes place at four different post positions. For example, the tenth target might be an 18-incher shot at from ranges of 45, 40, 35 and 30 yards. (Or, if terrain necessitates, a bowman might shoot at four different targets at those distances from a single post.) Archers shoot in the order of scores made at the previous target—high first, then second highest, etc. They go over the course in groups of four, give or take one. An archer who places all four arrows in the center ring of an 18- or 24-inch target in an NFAA-registered shoot gets the coveted 20-pin Award.

Because sight users may have an unfair advantage over bare-bow or instinctive men, those who use sights officially compete only against each other in a separate classification known as *free style*. (Sight users include even those who have a blemish on their bow used in aiming.)

Another classification is set according to ability. Initially based on the average score from an archer's first two tournament rounds, it increases as his tournament average increases. (In certain instances an archer may be reclassified downward, too. But the State Field Governor must approve.)

In addition to the Field Found, bowmen also shoot the Animal Round and the Hunter's Round. The Hunter's Round is a little tougher than the Field Round, more closely simulating the problems one might run into while hunting. Different stakes are used on the regular course (usually colored blue, occasionally red), and the bowman must change shooting position on every shot. If a single stake is used at the shooting post, the archer must alternate sides (with his foot touching the stake); if two stakes are used, he must shoot an arrow from each side of each; with four stakes, one arrow from each. Designers of Hunter's Round courses make it a point to include a good number of trees, bushes, etc., in the line of flight.

All-black targets are used in Hunter's Rounds, with three-inch white aiming spots. Except for color, they're identical with conventional field targets. Rings are separated by thin white lines, invisible from shooting positions. Scoring is the same as for the Field Round.

The third major round is the Animal Round, so called because the targets are prints of various animals. Scoring for these is determined on how close one comes to the center, but the "vital" area (bull's-eye) is oblong, while lower points are received for hitting anywhere between the center oval and the animal's outline.

Shooting at these targets varies from the conventional in that the bowman shoots only until he makes a strike, with a maximum of three arrows, none of which are shot from the same distance. If, for example, the shooter strikes an elk in a vital area with his first shot (first shots at elk are set at 70 yards), he gets 20 points; if in a non-vital area, 16 points. If he hits the center with his second arrow (now a distance of 60 yards) he receives 14 points. And so on down the line. Finally, if he strikes a low-scoring area with his last arrow he gets only 4 points.

Broadheads used to be used on this round. They are no longer permitted; they rip the targets and are extremely dangerous—particularly during tournaments, when non-archers may be wandering through the woods.

Incidentally, the Animal Round quickly separates basically target archers from field men—and the field men come out on top. Reason: a target archer more or less writes off his first few arrows, using them to sight in on a target. The instinctive archer, on the other hand, usually does quite well with his first few arrows, does progressively worse as time goes on.

PROFESSIONAL

After a couple of decades of talk, the Professional Archers Association (PAA) finally became a vital force in August, 1963, with the first National Tournament, held in Daytona Beach, Florida. For this, the Official PAA Round was used. Layout in this round, designed for spectators, is something like a double horseshoe, one inside the other, with 20 targets arranged in a crescent around the outer horseshoe, the shooters along the inner, and spectators in the center. Because of the large opening in the center, onlookers can either follow favorite archers as they shoot or stay in one place and see all archers as they come through, progressing along the targets.

The official PAA face is black with thin white scoring rings and a white aiming dot. Targets come in three sizes. Three arrows are shot at each target, each from a different distance. No distance is repeated. For "short" targets (16 to 30 yards), 14-inch faces are used; 22-inch faces are shot in "middle-range" targets (29 to 50 yards); and on "long" targets (47 to 65 yards) 30-inch faces are used. Arrows count 5, 4, and 3, with 300 points possible on the 20 targets.

MAIL TOURNAMENTS

Both the NFAA and the NAA sponsor mail matches, tournaments conducted through the post office. The purpose is to make tournament competition universal, to give even the guy who lives on a remote island the chance to compete. Matches usually are comprised of events carried on over a series of weeks or months. The NFAA, for example, conducts seven bare-bow mail tournaments during the months of April through October, plus two Free Style Division Tournaments for those who use sights.

Because rules for mail tournaments seem to change often, it would be prudent to check with the NAA or NFAA on what's currently happening.

Chapter 15

SHOOT-FOR-DISTANCE ARCHERY

THERE comes the time in every archer's life when he gets the urge to see how far he can shoot. Some of us yield, and if we ever locate the arrow, we find the walk to it quite impressive. And that's the whole object of flight shooting—to make that walk as notable as possible. Little accuracy, just distance.

Flight bows are shot in two general ways. The first is quite similar to that of the conventional: the flight man holds his bow with one hand, draws back the arrow with the other, points skyward, and lets 'er fly. But if you see a flight shooter at work, you'll not think he's after ducks. In the first place, the bows are tremendously heavy—a 100-pound implement is not considered outstanding by enthusiasts—and in order to pull it back the archer's physique must rival Charles Atlas'. Little thought is given to the anchor point, for the arrow is released a fraction before full draw—so the anchor as likely as not is breastbone high. And look at a flight man's face: You'll see none of the calm and composure target archers affect (or are supposed to); instead, the whole face is strained, the eyes squinted, the jaw set or the mouth agape.

That's one kind of flight shooting—with a handbow—the oldest and most widely used. The other style arose from an accident. In 1923, Professor Charles D. Curtis, superintendent of schools at Pembina, North Dakota, broke his arm.

Before, he had been a superb flight shooter, but his arm never regained its strength. Next year he showed up at the national tournament anyway, carrying an extraordinary bow, a real eye-stopper: heavy, cumbersome-looking, with the oddest handle his cohorts had ever seen.

His form was flabbergasting. Flopping down on the alfalfa, he braced his shoes on the bow, pulled his slim, streamlined arrow back with both hands, and whiffed it straight into the morning sun. When disturbed officials finally found Dr. Curtis' arrow, they discovered that he had broken the 300-yard "insurmountable barrier" for the first time in America.

Strangely, nothing in the rules prevented him from shooting flat on his back. But this was changed. In subsequent tournaments two separate events were scheduled: "Regular" —arrows shot with a handbow by an archer on his feet, and "Free Style"—arrows shot in any other way. That's still the way things work.

Flight archery seems easy—no particular aiming, no obvious regard for form, no special interest in consistency. But easy it's not. In the first place, you have to be strong for heavyweight bows in arms, shoulders, chest, back. Second, style is of the utmost importance (though forms vary), the important points being a steady draw and perfect release with no hesitations. That release is tricky. If no wind is blowing you must strike an elevation of 42 or 43 degrees. If the wind is coming at you, the elevation must be lowered a degree or two, depending on the airspeed. With a tail wind, the angle must be raised—and strangely, a strong back breeze doesn't give additional yardage; it pushes the vanes upright so the arrow falls shorter than it should. And if it's gusty, who knows? Field and target archers can still function when the weather's off. Not so in flight when you're going after records; if it isn't the wind it's the humidity, or temperature, or even altitude.

Even the time of day is at odds with you; no friendly Saturday afternoon matches. Too much breeze then. Instead, hardy flight men shoot right after sunrise, the less hearty ones just before the sun sinks.

One big problem for the beginning flight man is finding a place to practice. If you live in the city with no means of transportation, you have problems. But if you can get to the country, you're set (if your face is pleasant and you show an interest in farming). You'll need about 700 yards of clear space at least a couple of hundred feet wide. At this distance the arrows stick upright in the ground, making them easy to spot—if they don't lodge in trees, float away in creeks or disappear in haystacks. Due to their fragility, many break on impact with a pebble or hard lump of dirt, may even shatter at launch if released improperly. Never forget that this kind of shooting is dangerous, that because of the quick-release style, mis-shoots and wild arrows are not uncommon.

Equipment for flight archery is odd: the heaviest bows used in archery—as much as 137 pounds or more for handbows, up to 250 pounds for footbows—with the lightest arrows—as little as ⅓ ounce. A conventional archer can use skill to make up for slight defects in equipment. A flight man, in the main, can shoot only so far as his equipment will allow.

Most flight work today is being done with two kinds of handbows: One measures about 4¼ feet, uses 25-inch arrows *overdrawn* on a track 3 inches. This was the bow—a 137-pounder—used by Danny Lamore, a rangy truck driver from Porterville, Calif., when he established a new NAA record of 850.2 yards in 1959. (A half hour earlier, using a 54-in. fiberglass and maple footbow of 250 pounds, he broke the old NAA free-style record by nearly 50 yards, slinging his arrow 937.13 yards.) The other type handbow looks, to the inexperienced eye, like an exquisitely carved toy. A typical one may be only 41 inches long. But it pulls more than a hundred pounds.

A few years ago a good lemon or yew bow was not expected to shoot much more than a dozen times before breaking. Today's fiberglass-backed models (often of maple) ordinarily last for hundreds of shots. A good hand flight bow runs somewhere around $100.

So far as footbows are concerned, there aren't many of them around—mainly because all are painstakingly made by hand, and the danger of breakage is great. Footbows are somewhat longer than regular bows and considerably heavier; weights start at about 100 pounds. They're strapped to the feet, which rest in built-in stirrups, and require at least two people to string.

Though there are a few flight men who use a three-fingered draw, most use a shooting hook or leather flipper. The hook usually is a piece of plastic molded to fit the palm, with a projection extending between the thumb and forefinger. Into this is cut a notch to hold the string. The flipper is a strap of leather enclosing the first two fingers and coming up between the first finger and thumb. It's pressed by the thumb against the finger as the thumb holds the string in the hook notch. To release, the archer relaxes his thumb, the string slips out of the hook and the flipper flaps, letting the string go. Flight men claim they can get another 30 yards or so by using this or a similar device. Footbow shooters ordinarily use two hooks or flipper sets, one in each hand.

Bows are usually made by their shooters, but you can have them built specially for you by the Drake Archery Shop, Lakeside, Calif. Flight arrows are available from many large archery supply houses; they cost $3 each and up. Most flight shooters use Port Orford cedar arrows footed with beefwood, but a few lean toward aluminum. Odd point: a fine Port Orford cedar arrow may be good for only three or four shots, maybe only one; after that, distance may be decreased by a third. Why? Nobody is sure. A longer-lifetime wood is Longleaf yellow pine. It must be more than fifty and less than eighty years old, not too dry (as from an old roof), nor too wet (from a cellar timber, for example). Archers have found wood in old telephone poles, beams from collapsed houses, headboards from beds, and old cabinets. The best arrows are saved for tournaments. For practice, flight shooters use whatever is available, so long as it is of the right weight and length. Flu-flus would be excellent for foot-weary flight men, but they can't be shot with an overdraw.

The arrows are almost always of barreled construction, swelling from $\frac{1}{8}$-inch or $\frac{5}{32}$-inch brass point to a $\frac{5}{16}$-inch midsection, then shrinking to a $\frac{1}{4}$-inch or smaller nock. They're usually available from 16 inches to 28 inches. The short, low-cut vanes—almost always of plastic—are set on straight; no energy-absorbing arrow spin is desired in flight archery. The tiny vanes are to give as little air resistance as possible, and the shaft's barrel shape combines sturdiness with lightness. One thing you don't have to worry about: matching. Flight arrows needn't be, shouldn't be, in fact. Best is a combination of various weights, with not too great a spread.

Though the great distances are the ones shouted about, one needn't be a mooselike mass of muscles to participate in flight archery. Men and women have different divisions, and youngsters are categorized by age and sex for a variety of other divisions. The women's and junior divisions shoot bows in the 35-pound, 50-pound, and unlimited classes (any size bows), as well as the free-style or footbow class. Men's classes are 50, 65 and 80 pounds, and unlimited, along with the free style. America's records are those set at the NAA National, so all serious flight men of necessity are NAA members.

In the whole history of American flight shooting, only one man—Charles Pierson—has won all classes, and that was in 1956 at Lakewood, New Jersey.

Flight archery technology has a good distance to go. Nobody in the know thinks we've reached anywhere near the distance of which we are capable. Experimentation involving wood/plastic relationships is needed, research in optimum power ratios to length is called for, even new strings must be developed (they last for only about six shots now). This is a wide-open field, and those interested in bow design and the physics of archery might find research and development in flight archery rewarding.

Records are being broken, but not as quickly as they might be. Soon we'll probably cross the thousand-yard mark, but the sixteenth-century Turks are said to have hit this distance on many occasions, as ancient markers still in the old flight fields testify.

As a matter of fact, it was a little, unassuming Turk who made the first great flight shot of modern times—one that wasn't beaten by the West for 144 years. In 1795 Mahmoud Effendi, secretary to the Turkish Ambassador to England, hauled back a reflex, composite bow made in his hometown, modestly flung the arrow 480 yards. (He said that in his homeland this distance was almost embarrassing.) Not until 1939 did any Westerner beat him shooting a handbow—and that was C. A. "Pop" Bowman of El Paso, Texas, who finally punctured existing records during the Western Archery Association Tournament in Phoenix, Ariz., with a distance of 483 yards 4 inches.

Only once to our knowledge have the ancient Turks' records been bettered. This is how Dr. Robert P. Elmer tells it in his classic *Archery:*

> Undoubtedly the longest flight shot of which there remains a record so authentic that it can be accepted without a quibble was that of the Persian archer named Aresh, who stood on top of the mountain Damovend and, just as the sun peeped over the horizon, loosed a shaft with such splendid vigor that it did not strike the earth until sunset, when it landed in the banks of the river Gihon about five hundred miles away.

Chapter 16

CLOUT, GOLF AND OTHER ARCHERY ODDITIES

THE Indians, so it is said by the Indians, were great at turtle shooting. They wouldn't aim directly at the turtles, but loosed their arrows toward the sun. The missiles would turn round on themselves and fly down smack into the turtles, skewering them to logs. So they say.

Similar to the Indian turtle shoot is the ancient round of clout, getting its name from the Old English *clut*, which meant "patch." A white rag tied to a stick or stretched on a frame made up the first clout target. Clout shooting is a giant form of archery: target dimension figures are identical to those of regular target archery, but they refer to feet instead of inches. Therefore, instead of having a 9.6-inch center with a total target diameter of 48 inches, the gold is 9.6 *feet* across, the outer target diameter 48 feet. The whole thing is laid out flat on the ground. Lines between the rings are themselves about two inches wide.

The distance to the target is 180 yards for men, 140 (ordinarily) for women. Scoring is the same as in regular target archery. Often two targets are used—one at each end of the field. Cuts walking in half.

The first authorized American clout shoot took place at Cooperstown, N.Y., in 1922, and though today there are few

187

specialists clouting, the shoot has remained a diverting part of national tournaments. Three things make it particularly interesting: 1) the beauty of an arrow arching off into the distance, 2) the difficulty in judging just the right angle of launch, and 3) the "handicap" working against all participating shooters—experienced and beginner alike—in the form of luck, principally injected by playful wind currents.

Standard tackle is used, but it must be fairly heavy; lighter bows may not be able to dispatch arrows all the way to the target. In non-official clouting, a gentlemen's agreement often is that the distance to the target center equals the cast of the weakest bow among the shooters. This gives a healthy advantage to the man with the lightweight bow; he's concerned only with direction at full draw, not distance.

So far as his competitors are concerned, distance is varied not by the draw, but by the launch angle. To better judge this angle, some cloutmen put a strip of adhesive tape on the lower arm of their bows, marked either with angle or distance, found through trial and error. To see this mark more easily, some have effected a chest draw, the anchor point falling on the breastbone.

A clout round consists of six ends of six arrows each. If an arrow hits a rock and falls over, the point's resting place determines the value (assuming the point is still attached to the arrow). Accuracy at this range can be surprising. Scores of 250 (the equivalent of about half in the orange, half in the gold) are not uncommon.

An offshoot of standard clout—advocated by those who consider themselves primarily field, rather than target, archers—is called *battle clout*. Main difference is that the target is farther—200 yards, and larger—center 12 feet wide, with a total target diameter of 60 feet. Broadheads often are used, ⅞ of an inch wide or larger, with a total arrow weight of at least 425 grains, or about 13 grains less than an ounce. Scoring and number of arrows shot are the same as in conventional clouting.

Another interesting change-of-pace game is archery golf. Less strenuous than either target or field archery, it seems to lend itself more to whole family participation. Unfortunately, finding a course is not too easy; seems that golfers have a curious aversion to arrows flying while they're putting.

The object of archery golf is the same as in regular golf— get around the course with the least number of "strokes"— with two main differences: archers don't sink their putts, but strike tiny targets; and where golfers use a variety of clubs and the same ball, archers use a single bow, different arrows.

For some reason, archery golf is exceedingly popular in the West, particularly the Northwest, but as of this writing, no large-scale course is open on the East Coast. In the West, the game is played with strict-rule seriousness; on make-do eastern courses, it's mainly a way to get away from serious competition, with the participants varying their rules with the course. If played on a regular golf course, golfers sometimes are challenged to a round or two, induced by handicaps.

At first glance, archery golf seems relatively new. It's not. If looked at broadly (as a derivative of roving), it's the oldest form of archery. An ancient bowman didn't bother with regulation bull's-eye targets, but shot at anything that happened to strike his fancy—an old stump, a clump of weeds, a visiting tribesman. Many archery historians, in fact, believe that golf itself is a direct descendant of roving, that if there were no such thing as archery, golf also would be missing. One old archery writer suggested that British Islanders found it cheaper to substitute crooked sticks, thistle balls, and holes for tackle and target butts. At any rate, the first authenticated archery-golf game in America played under that name took place in 1910, as reported in the November 30, 1912 issue of *Forest and Stream*. And periodically it has been popping up as a "great new sport" ever since.

What kind of course do you need? Best is a standard golf

course, but lacking this, any large area will do. Distances of targets should be mixed and include anything from 30 to 300 or more yards. "Holes" consist of 4-inch balls of excelsior or thread-wrapped cotton. The National Field Archery Association suggests attaching a 3-inch "handling loop" to the ball, then dipping the whole thing in Latex Number 16 (sold by, among others, George R. Cummings, Jr. Co. of Cincinnati, St. Louis and Milwaukee). Some sort of tee on which to set the targets is helpful—a straight hunk of fairly stiff wire, for example. Players are forever trying to putt from too-far distances, and when they miss a teed target, the arrows skid for a considerable distance on the other side. Some players rule out hits that splash sand and knock off the target.

The NFAA recommends that players on a make-do course come equipped with a pocketful of 20-inch stakes, either painted white or with flags attached, these to mark shooting positions and target locations. Place targets whenever possible on hazards—knolls or the edge of banks—where a miss means a long shot back. If a regular golf course is used, a good idea is to place targets just off the green, so the well-manicured grass won't be hacked up by divoting arrows.

No special equipment is needed for archery golf, but some large mail-order houses (Kittredge Bow Hut in South Pasadena, Calif., for example) sell sets that include one flight arrow, an approach arrow with non-skid point, and a blunt "putter" arrow, all of which are designed to take a maximum of abuse. A putting arrow can be improvised by sliding a cartridge shell over a standard pile, or by wrapping the point with tape. In winter, aluminum flight arrows should be used; wooden ones will break on the frozen ground.

Nobody has yet set down hard rules for archery golf, but these are some advocated by the NFAA: 1) No preliminary practice is allowed. 2) Each man shoots an arrow from the tee, then during the next round, the one *farthest* from the target shoots first, then the second farthest, etc. 3) On all shots except the tee, players shoot from wherever their arrows lie. 4) A hit is credited when the arrow lands within an arrow's length of the target ball, or when the ball is knocked from its stake. 5) If an arrow is lost, an extra point is added, the next shot being made from the nearest point of disappearance.

Par for a nine-holer, if a golf course is used, is nine under par. Nice thing about the game is that even the first time out a novice can get a fairly good score.

Along with clout shooting and archery golf, a number of other offbeat archery activities have been devised—some as old as the sport itself, others new as the telescopic bow sight. One of the oldest:

WAND SHOOT, in which 36 arrows are shot at a softwood "wand" 2 inches wide and 6 feet high. Men shoot at 100 yards, women at 60. The wand shoot first was placed on the official schedule in 1922 at Cooperstown, N. Y. (same year and place as the clout shoot's introduction), but actually has been around for centuries, the original target consisting of a 2-inch-thick peeled sapling trunk. A good wand shoot practice target consists of a 2-inch strip of adhesive tape running down the center of a target butt. If you make your own wooden target, be sure that it is well braced; otherwise the weight of the arrows sticking in it may cause it to teeter forward, snapping off wooden shafts.

HIT AND DROP BACK is one of a number of archery activities loosely categorized as novelty shoots. Such diversions serve a couple of useful purposes. For one thing they usually give second-besters a chance to rank in score with better men than they. For another, they add variety. And novelty shoots are good moneymaking activities for clubs. The hit-and-drop, however, is no money-maker; its main import is that it gives the novice a fighting chance. The game is played over a regular field course, and the gimmick is that whenever anyone hits the target, he must take three backward paces (18 feet or so) for his next shot. In rough terrain, you get into some interesting situations shooting with your fourth arrow.

In a BALLOON SHOOT a number of air, and gas-filled balloons are secreted in the kinds of places in which game might be hiding. When released, they act as moving targets. (Only flu-flu arrows are practical when gas-filled balloons are used.)

TURKEY SHOOT is another typical novelty game. In this, for a set entry fee, contestants try their skill (and luck) with a predetermined number of arrows for a real turkey while shooting at a fake one. Everyone who can hit the broadside of a turkey is in the running, for from the firing line, numbered sections can't be seen. Other targets used in turkey shoots: vari-colored, oddly numbered cut-out pictures; swinging pendulums (the archer's arrow stops them from swinging and counts for whatever number is written on the pendulum where it comes to rest against the arrow); balloons with numbers inside, including minus numbers; cut-out numbers hidden behind newspapers; endless-chain-drawn targets (cranked by hand or run from an auto battery and motor); hay bales spinning on an overhead rope, with targets on all four sides; and a William Tell target, where the apple counts 10, the boy's head (fake) minus 10 (a headful of arrows is a sight to remember).

MIDWAY SHOOT is another good fund-raiser. For predetermined prizes, each archer pays a quarter or so for, say, six arrows, and shoots at an offbeat target. When the croupier gathers the price of the prize, plus a little left over for the club, he calls a halt, and the top scorer walks off with the goods.

CANOE SHOOT, a recent addition to the novelty field, works like this: Targets are placed along the shores of a river—the more swiftly flowing the better. Archers compete in pairs. One paddles while his partner shoots for half the course, then they change jobs for the second half. Boats leave the starting point at five-minute intervals—time to allow each target's official to add scores and remove arrows before the next boat comes along.

One other kind of shoot must be mentioned. It's not very popular now, nor is it likely to sweep the country. It does, however, require fantastic skill:

HORSEBACK ARCHERY, similar to the canoe shoot but practiced in the Southwest in preparation for hunting jack rabbits, javelina, and peccaries. At full gallop the archer whizzes past and shoots at butts strewn around a field, a technique taking a crack archer and a hot-shot rider. But it's easier than desert horseback hunting; at least the butts aren't jumping across the countryside.

Chapter 17

CROSSBOWS

IT may seem strange to find a section on the cross-bow in an archery book, but somehow it belongs—despite the fact that the weapon's on-shoulder stock, trigger, and accurate front and rear sights make a crossbow seem more like a rifle than a bow. Although it acts like a rifle, the weapon does use an arrow, however, and nearly all cross-bow enthusiasts either are former long bowmen or have a good working knowledge of archery.

Essentially, the crossbow consists of a short, fairly heavy bow made of wood, metal, or fiberglass and mounted cross-wise on a riflelike stock. On American models the string is drawn with both hands by resting the stock against the chest, and hooked in the drawn position before the arrow is put in place. A trigger arrangement releases the string, and the arrow starts its journey in a groove running along the top of the stock. Accuracy ordinarily is about twice that of con-ventional bows. And it's always been so, even back in the ninth century, when isolated crossbows first popped up.

Nobody knows for sure how crossbows originated, but the theory is that an occasional longbowman would turn his bow onto its side, fashion a shoulder-rest stock to its center for stability, hook the string over a notch in the stock, and lay the arrow in a groove on top. A hole through the stock with a stick poking up against the string gave him a trigger. He could take his time sighting, for once the weapon was drawn, he had no need to concern himself with holding the string back. When on the mark, he'd jiggle the stick and the string would jump from the notch, sending the arrow on its way.

Crossbows began to become important as military weapons early in the eleventh century. They held two main advantages: extreme accuracy and ease of operation—a good man needed only days, or at the most, weeks, to learn to shoot a crossbow, while it required months or even years to train a crack longbowman.

Crossbows had two main drawbacks, however. They were expensive, unlike simple longbows. And they were slow. According to one historical report, it took up to 10 minutes for a fast crossbowman to load and loose his weapon, while longbowmen steadily rained arrows down on him. Long loading time can be understood when you realize that some of the bows had draws approaching a thousand pounds and, not surprisingly, had to be wound up with a crank. In 1139, the Lateran Council in Rome banned use of the crossbow for Christian warfare, expressing the opinion that it was a weapon ". . . hateful to God and unfit for Christians. . . ." The infidels, however, unimpressed by the judgment, kept right on using them. Soon crossbows were widely employed all across Europe and Asia Minor.

Kings and emperors kept changing their minds about the crossbows—at one time promoting their use, at another issuing edicts forbidding them. But then gunpowder appeared and the argument became academic; both crossbows and longbows gradually were eased out. The crossbow, incidentally, helped in the evolution of hand firearms; the stock was easily adapted to support a barrel.

Today, of course, crossbows are used only for sport, though both the U.S. and Australian armed services considered employing them as silent weapons for use during World War II jungle fighting. No evidence is available that crossbows were actually used in modern combat.

America currently is seeing a revived interest in sports crossbows, centering around three principal associations: The National Crossbowmen (headquartered in Cranford, N. J.), The American Crossbow Association (Huntsville, Arkansas), and The National Company of Crossbowmen (Coronado, Calif.). Most crossbowmen who compete for honors at the annual NAA National are members of The National Crossbowmen; the ACA and NCC hold their own tournaments. Each national association is composed of regional groups.

As practiced in the Western world today, crossbow shooting is almost exclusively a target, rather than hunting, sport. The only state in the U.S. that allows crossbow hunting (the season is very brief) is Arkansas. And the situation doesn't

Typical American-style crossbow, assembled and in carrying case. This one was built by Fred Isles, president of The National Crossbowmen.

seem to be changing. The main reason is that crossbowmen don't care; they're content to shoot at inanimate targets.

Incidentally, there's a persistent rumor to the effect that in New Jersey it is illegal even to *own* a crossbow. Where this started is unknown, but it has no basis in fact. The only law that anyone has been able to trace pertains to prohibition *for hunting* of "spring" guns, of which a crossbow is certainly an example.

The modern American crossbow differs somewhat from its European cousin, as does the style of shooting. Basically, the American bow is lighter, the bowman more casual. The average native bow weighs around 7 or 8 pounds, has a pull of between 40 and 80 pounds, and draws from 16 to 20 inches. Material usually is of solid or laminated fiberglass, casting arrows at about 200 feet per second. Under American rules the bow must be hand drawn rather than pulled by lever in the European style.

A typical European crossbow weighs somewhere between about 14 and 40 pounds, and the steel bow often has a draw weight approaching 200 or 300 pounds. A lever, of course, is needed for cocking.

Crossbow arrows are about half the length of conventional arrows, often a little fatter. They may be of wood, aluminum, or fiberglass, with feathers or plastic vanes. They have no nocks. Correctly, they're *bolts* or *darts*. (Few archers in this country, however, call them anything other than arrows.) *Quarrels* is a common misnomer. These actually are special arrows with four-cornered points, intended to pierce armor plate.

Incidentally, the phrase "bolt from the blue" doesn't refer to lightning but to crossbow bolts, stemming from the ancient war practice of shooting them in high arcs, something like modern mortar fire. Likewise, "bolt upright" comes from the straightness for which arrows are noted, as evidenced by this quotation from Chaucer's *Miller's Tale*: "She was long as a mast, and uprighte as a bolt." And while we're

In most of central Europe crossbow shooting is more widely practiced than conventional archery. Here, in a typical Swiss meet, archers shoot at 60 targets.

on it, the phrase "to pick a quarrel," according to one historian, means that one should select a particularly fine crossbow projectile before meeting one's enemy.

Swiss bolts, by the way, really do look like bolts. Ordinarily just under six inches long and a half inch in diameter, they're featherless, with a threaded, screw-type point. Each crossbow has only one arrow (and perhaps a spare) matched to it. After the Swiss crossbowman's single shot, his partner *unscrews* the bolt from the wooden or lead target, and on regulation ranges, places the bolt in a basket supported by a wire and zips it via trolley back to the shooter.

An American crossbowman takes a stance similar to that used by conventional archers. His Swiss counterpart uses three cushions, kneeling on one with his right knee, placing another under the instep of his right foot, a third atop his right foot. Then he sits on this third cushion, and rests his left elbow on his upright left knee. Uncomfortable, till you get used to it. But marvelously sturdy. NAA rules, on the other hand, state that American crossbowmen must stand to shoot, can use no rests. In the old country, the target often is a 4-inch post set on end in the center of a 12-inch target. Occasionally an 8-inch face is used. A European face consists of ten circles.

To string an American crossbow, the archer uses either of two methods. The first method is this: Loop one eye around one of the crossbow's limbs, pulling the loop over and past the bow nock. Put the other loop in the nock of the other arm. Then placing the butt of the stock on the ground between your feet, grab the bow ends, lean down on them, and work the loose loop into the nock.

The other method uses a "bracing" string, a cord somewhat longer than the regular string. The short regular string is placed on the limbs first, in one nock and past the nock a bit on the other limb. Then the bracing string is slipped over the bow's tips, drawn back to the catch (where the trigger mechanism pokes through the stock tops) and slipped over. The bow is bent enough now so that the shorter string can easily be slipped into the nocks. When the aid string is removed the bow springs back, stretching the final string tight.

Crossbows are cocked by bracing the butt against the chest, hauling back on the string with both hands to the string release slot. A few shooters use crossbows with cross-bolts or screw eyes in the nose of their weapons. These snap over hooks on footheld stands, so that the bowman can pull the string using his back muscles as well as his arms.

The arrow is placed in the barrel groove with the cock feather down. The weapon is sighted like a rifle through a peep or notch sight, or on some models, both—but no telescopic sights are allowed in American competitions. Usually the crossbow simply rests against the shooter's shoulder (there's remarkably little recoil), but in Europe, larger and heavier crossbows often are steadied on made-to-fit firing benches.

Almost all crossbowmen—particularly in this country—are also rather skilled home craftsmen. Good thing, because if you want a good crossbow you'll probably have to make it. For years, U.S. crossbowmen got their weapons from a New Jerseyite named Harry L. Bailey—pioneer inventor and popularizer of the modern target crossbow in America. All existing crossbow national records are held either by Bailey-built crossbows or close copies of them.

Since Bailey's death in 1961, there's only one really fine commercial American crossbow maker, in the opinion of many top crossbowmen: George Stevens of Huntsville, Arkansas.

If you want to make your own, excellent plans for building a Bailey-type target crossbow are available at $5 a set from The National Crossbowmen, 10 Arlington Road, Cranford, N.J. As George Stevens says, "More tournaments are won in the workshop than on the shooting line."

In tournaments, crossbowmen shoot alongside, but not in competition with, longbowmen. A two-foot target is used, half the standard size. Using the smaller target, crossbowmen average about the same scores as conventional shooters using double-size targets, indicating that a crossbow's inherent accuracy is about twice that of a conventional bow. A good crossbowman can place nearly all the arrows inside a 9-inch circle at 40 yards, with maybe half of these hitting in the 4.8-inch gold.

Crossbowmen participate in every phase of tournament archery, including clout, wand, and flight. Flight record at this time for a crossbow is 668 yards (compared with 937 yards for a foot-drawn flight bow). Says Fred Isles, president

Fred Isles cocks his crossbow (right) and prepares to shoot at frontyard target.

of The National Crossbowmen: "We're going to beat that, going to beat it by a very large margin. We have the materials now—wonderful materials—and there's no reason in the world why we shouldn't go way over a thousand."

But perhaps more than in any other aspects of archery, the *participation* counts more than the *results*. As President Isles explains, "Crossbows are especially good for longbowmen like me who no longer have their old stamina. The crossbow is an ideal way of keeping up an association with old friends. That, to us, is what matters—not to hit the mark necessarily, but to be out there on the field with these people we have known for years."

Chapter 18

FISHING WITH A BOW

THE first time you try bowfishing, the experience will tax your patience. The short distance to the game—10 to 20 feet or so—makes bowfishing seem a snap. But the quarry is not where it appears to be, and your arrows won't go where they should. Light refraction plays strange tricks. Heavy arrows dragging fishlines make odd flight patterns. Flight is altered even more when the arrow strikes the water. In addition, the bowfisherman's footing is most likely to be far from solid: if he isn't on a pitching boat deck, he's on a slippery mud bank; if not on a wobbly dock, then climbing alga-covered rocks.

On the other hand, fishing with a bow is exciting—as stimulating, say bowfishermen, as hunting small game with a rifle. It combines the qualities of field work and target shooting, adds the fascination of hunting and fishing. Fish aren't so dumb after all, and it takes a smart hunter to stalk them, a good archer to hit them. What's more, the sport is safe and cheap.

Recently bowfishing has seen a revival among American archers. But it isn't at all new: Nearly any large museum exhibits cleverly designed fishing arrows once used by South Sea Islanders, Eskimos and Indians.

One big hang-up to modern bowfishing is that in many places it's illegal. This policy is changing, however, and most states now have some kind of season open for at least "rough" fish—gar, carp, suckers, mudfish (bowfins), eel.

You'll probably need a fishing license, no matter what your game. Check with your local fish and game commission, or your expedition may be marred by a heavy fine plus stiffer irritation. A note to your state commissioner will bring a quick answer. Addresses are listed in the Appendix.

Hardly a fish has been exempt from being taken by bow-fishermen, and that includes sting rays, shark, even marlins. But to most bowmen, *the* fish is carp. During egg-laying time the females swim into marshes, backwater pools, and mud flats so shallow at times their backs stick out of the water as they wallow and flop in the mud. Shooting them then is no trick. In midsummer, however, after the fish have returned to deeper waters, the carp-hunter is surprised at just how wily and strong the critters can be. Another surprise for the inexperienced: the size. Carp often run to 20 pounds and a yard long; in 1961 a 48-pound monster was bagged in Michigan by a bowfisherman, the biggest carp ever caught in that state by any method.

Most impressive fish-shoot to date was performed by that all round archery expert Howard Hill, while cruising with Errol Flynn through Mexican waters. With his first shot the Hollywood bowman struck a marlin in the brain, knocking him stone dead. His second shot got another marlin between the dorsal fin and the head—not deep enough to kill, but enough to hold tight. The battle lasted for more than an hour and a half and finally ended when the marlin rushed the skiff, hit with such force that he broke completely through one side, stopped when his sword pierced the opposite gunwale. (For those who know fishing: Hill coaxed marlin to the surface with Zane Grey teasers, used a 30-foot hunk of piano wire as leader, running line to a No. 14 Covaleski reel on a bamboo rod.)

Few archers will have an opportunity to shoot marlin. But for most, carp are enough. Equipment needed, in addition to the bow: fishing arrow, simple reel, line. Total cost: about $5. Line must occasionally be replaced and rocks will smash a few points, but aside from such accidents, a good set of tackle should last the bowfisherman for years.

BOWS used for fishing are conventional. Use your target or hunting bow. A typical fishing bow is the 51-pound Bear Cub with which forty-one-year-old Gene Reilly of Wormleysburg, Pa., nailed a 50-pound, 2-ounce carp in 1963, biggest bow-speared freshwater fish of that year. For gar, you'll need a fairly large bow to penetrate thick scales—a minimum of 55 pounds or so.

Because a bow might take a beating around the water, some fishermen save their expensive implement for hunting or target shooting, and use a cheap fiberglass model for water work. Many fishers wrap their bows with wide masking tape or coat them with stick-camouflage to cut down on fish-frightening glare.

POINTS for arrows present a problem. More than 70 different kinds are sold and at least one more decade will have to pass before bowfishing experience has sorted out best and runners-up. The best idea is to try a few—whatever your local shop is pushing—and see what happens. Some fishermen get around the problem (or increase it) by designing their own. Essential considerations number two: 1) the point—ordinarily with a hole drilled through—must be rugged enough to puncture heavy scales; 2) it must be barbed. Opinions differ as to the best arrangement—one or two barbs. But it is agreed that barbs should either be flexible or foldable, so that when the point enters the fish's body the barbs close tight against the shank, open again inside the fish.

Cheaper points have stationary barbs—just as good to spear fish, but devilishly difficult to extricate. With stationary-barbed points you must either cut it from the fish or push the arrow through and cut the line.

The best arrow heads are those with depressible barbs, folded to the shaft either by twisting the arrow or sliding a collar toward the head. This either forces the barbs closed inside the fish or allows them to slip forward. In either case, withdrawal is easier.

SHAFTS for bowfishing must be waterproof and should be heavier than conventional arrows if used in deeper waters. Some bowmen simply use cast-off wooden shafts and give them a half-dozen coats of thin varnish to prevent warping. Such shafts are too light for much water penetration, however. Better material is fiberglass—the solid kind, not tubing. Not only has glass sufficient weight, but it is waterproof and virtually indestructible. For saltwater work when the quarry is shark or ray, steel rods usually are used. At least one man is using a cut-up television antenna.

Fishing arrows usually are longer than those used for hunting; 30 inches is about average. This allows for weird points, odd nocks, etc. The draw remains the same.

FLETCHING on seagoing arrows, if used at all, must be waterproof. And there is some question as to whether it actually is needed. Waterproof vanes are quite heavy, and the increased flight stability may or may not make up for the added weight. At short distances—to 25 feet or so—vanes probably are superfluous; the line dragging behind does the job.

For long shots, however, vanes are needed. Though good

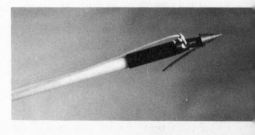

Rubber-fletched, fiberglass arrow with barbed point is typical for fishing. Here, line is attached directly to point; usually a one-foot metal leader runs between the point and the line.

Equipment courtesy Bear Archery Co.

plastic fletching is now being developed, rubber is still the best waterproof material. Rubber vanes molded in three-feather units provide the do-it-yourself archer a shortcut to fish arrow making. The units slip over the unfeathered shaft end. If conventional feathers are used, they must be coated heavily with some waterproofing material (available from mail-order retailers)—and still won't last long.

Another type of fletching is a small, sliding plastic ring—something like those used on potholders, but heavier. The line attaches to the ring as it rests near the bow hand, and as the arrow is loosed, the ring slides up to the nock and stops against a pin. Most archers find this arrangement troublesome, but a few use nothing else. The only time I tried it the pin broke off as the arrow sped on to the fish, hit it, and disappeared, fish and all, beneath the waves.

REELS come in a variety of types and sizes. Fortunately, they're all simply constructed and rather inexpensive. One archer, in fact, used a plastic drinking cup as his reel in a recent "carp-pinning" contest and walked off with third prize. The cup was screwed to a narrow board about five inches long, which in turn was taped to the bow just below the handle. He wrapped the fishline around the cup, tied one end through a hole near the bottom.

This homemade rig is not so unconventional as it seems. Most commercial models work on the same principle: a cylinder or cone is taped to the bow (no screws) either above or below the handle. Usually it has a raised lip to prevent the line from slipping off all at once. The line runs from the end of the reel rather than the top or bottom.

An adaptation is the "shoot through" type, a hollow reel of diameter large enough so the arrow actually travels through it. Manufacturers of this claim greater flight stability. The increased diameter does make it easier to rewind.

Some fishermen tape a regular spinning reel to the bow with the handle on the side opposite from the arrow rest.

Most archers find the added weight disturbing, even though a mechanical rewind is nice to have along. Another disadvantage is that in the heat of fish pursuit you might forget to press the release button before loosing, and a snagged line can easily snap the arrow back at you. Because of this possibility, many fish shooters wear gloves on their bow hands. A gloved hand also prevents line burns when playing a fish.

One interesting reel looks something like old-time kite-string reels: a coffee-cup-size unit with a handle on the back. This isn't attached to the bow, but held in the bow hand. After the arrow has found its mark, the bow is set down on the ground, and the fish played with the handheld reel. Similar to this method is one used for big game fish, impossible to handle with a conventional bow reel. A seafaring bowfisher uses his bow to implant the arrow, but a 15-yard coil of line sits on the seat beside him, leading to a conventional rod and reel. Often two people work the unit—one handling the bow, the other the reel.

LINES used for bowfishing are standard tangle-resistant fishing line. Test strength can be anywhere from about 40 to 90 pounds, depending on the kind of fish stalked. Braided nylon is best, and sports stores know the strength needed for local fish. Less than 40-pound test line should not be used for bowfishing—not necessarily because fish will part it, but because that extra strength is needed to drag arrows out of the mud. Sixty feet of line is a good minimum. Seems a lot, but remember, no rod is used to play the fish. For hard fighting or running game, even more is advisable.

When the bow is all set for a shot the line passes from the reel through a small hole near the end of the arrow, then is tied to a foot-long "seven-strand" type braided wire leader of 90 pounds test. A metal leader is recommended because some fish scales are sharp as razors and can cut through line like cheese. The leader-line junction usually is taped to the shaft to keep it from flopping.

The line must be secured to the nock end, else the arrow

would be affected in flight by the weight of the unrolling line. But it should not be tied only to the nock, or a big fish could merely roll over, break the arrow, and you'd be left not only fishless but pointless. Some fishermen secure the line to the nock end by a single layer of cellophane tape. After the arrow has sped home, the line easily cuts through this tape and rewind pressure can be exerted directly on the point.

Into-water archery presents an interesting visual problem: Unless the shooter is directly over his quarry, he doesn't aim at it. The fish isn't where it appears to be. When light at an angle passes through media of different densities—air and water in this case—it refracts (bends) so that a pole thrust into the water at an angle appears to be broken where it cuts the surface. You can see refraction at work by a simple experiment. Place a coin in a coffee can, then move back until it is hidden by the rim. Fill the can with water, and the image of the coin will move into your range of vision.

Because of refraction, fish appear to be slightly farther away and nearer the surface than they actually are. So the bowfisherman aims below the image, a distance varied in proportion to the fish's depth and the angle at which it is seen. How much? Judgment is gained only through experience, but a rule of thumb might be to underaim about the same distance that the fish *appears* to be deep. One West Coast archery school teaches students to aim by filling colored balloons with varying amounts of water, placing the balloons at various distances and depths in a pond, and letting the students fire at will.

Refraction isn't the only tricky factor. Almost as exasperating to the fishing novice is the flight of the arrow. It just doesn't act right. Heavier shaft and fletching and dragging line cause the cast to be considerably shortened. And after one shot the line is wet, adding more weight, more problems.

Now that we're rolling, let's add another ointment fly: the path of the arrow is dramatically affected when it hits the water. It's deflected downward when it strikes, the angle

Bowfishing combines the qualities of hunting and fishing, with archery, but is not as easy as it seems; the arrow doesn't act as it does in target work.

Equipment courtesy Bear Archery Co.

varying mainly with the distance from the shooter, up to 40 feet or so. Beyond that the arrow will likely skip across the surface. Obviously, the bowfisherman is by necessity an "instinctive" archer; he can't use point-of-aim, and a sight won't help much either.

Technique in shooting on the water is more like hunting than fishing. You see the game before you try for it. If you're shooting from a bank, the secret, of course, is to spot the fish before it spies you. Don't wear white clothing or you won't get away with it. Walk stealthily, or better, stand still. Some bowmen claim it's better to have the sun at your back so you won't be bothered by reflection. Most, however, find that the light should come from the front, so that the shadow won't scare the fish and the outline won't be silhouetted against the sky.

To counteract reflection and false shadows, a pair of polarized sunglasses is a big help. Also handy, suggests Charles Montana, president of The Watchung Bowmen, is binoculars. His technique is to stand high on a bank, glass the water carefully, then head for the highest concentration of fish. Incidentally, Montana swears that he once shot a carp so large that when the line was tied to his rowboat, the fish towed him up and down the river.

In some cases you can lure the fish to the surface. Bait can be bread hunks, chopped-up fish, hamburger or earthworms, depending on what you have on hand and what kind of fish you're after. Don't shoot at the first nose that appears. That belongs to the inexperienced youngster.

Bowfishing in many areas has a bad name. The main reason is a combination of laws limiting the kind of fish allowed to be taken by bow and arrow, and bowfishermen themselves. Because most of the fish legally shot are so-called "rough" fish—carp, suckers, gar—that to most Americans are inedible, archers in many cases simply leave them to rot on the banks.

Some of these fish are surprisingly good if cooked correctly. In Europe, in fact, carp is accepted as a standard table fish, though if improperly prepared it can be bony and strong flavored. A good cookbook can tell you how to prepare carp filet so the fish won't be greasy or strong. Even suckers can be tasty if they have grown up in clean water and are well prepared. (Sorry, there's not much hope for gar.)

If you just don't like fish, other disposal methods are available. A little asking around might reveal a few fish-hungry neighbors. Or if you have a backyard vegetable garden, bury the fish—old Indian method of fertilization. Or if you don't want to bring them home, slit their bellies with a knife and either bury them on the bank or shove them under foliage growing along the shore.

If you ever get bored with freshwater rough fish, try something really rough: shark. One archer who did was Dr. Leroy Bates, a San Antonio surgeon. According to Dr. Bates, "Every surgeon knows that a round needle will not go through tough skin," so he filed chisel-like ends on ⅜-inch aluminum rods, fashioned arrows from these. Deciding that no practical line would hold a shark, he attached a float to his arrow line. For bait he took along two gallons of beef blood preserved with anticoagulant and penicillin.

In the Bahamas, Dr. Bates and a couple of fellow archers not only bagged four sharks but a four-foot sting ray and twenty-odd varieties of other fish. He discovered that regular fishing arrows bounce off shark hide, but that conventional broadheads penetrate quite well, and the doctor's chisel-ended rods even better. He suggests, however, that the best method is to attach points to fiberglass shafts with brads; all of his screw-on heads were lost. He also found that no arrow was effective against fish deeper than about five feet.

Though Dr. Bates has fished from Mexico to Alaska, hunting extensively all along the southwest gulf area, "No hunting or fishing trip I have ever taken was as much pure fun" as the Bahama bowsharking venture, he said.

Chapter 19

ARROWSMITHERY

ODD, isn't it, how quickly the box of damaged arrows grows. Hit the target each time you draw, and your missiles will last for months. But breathes there an archer with eye so clear, and arm so set, and loose so smooth that it can never be said that instead of the target he bulled a rock?

The rack of good arrows dwindles, while the pile of bad mounts. Eventually every archer wonders—as he plunks down a dollar each for new arrows—if he wouldn't save money by making his own.

Indeed he would—and as he learns the craft of fletching, he begins to appreciate just what constitutes a good arrow.

Fortunately, one needn't begin in these enlightened times by splitting a log and decapitating a turkey. Well-stocked stores and mail-order houses handle basic parts—shafts, fletching, nocks, points—as well as tools. The modern do-it-yourselfer can make a set of nicely matched wooden arrows for something like $4 worth of materials (exclusive of tools).

You can buy fine Port Orford cedar shafts, for example, for less than $2 a dozen, or about $13 per hundred. (One seller: Craftsman Wood Service Co., 2727 S. Mary Street, Chicago 8, Ill.) It's doubtful that you could make your own shafts for this amount—if your time is worth anything—and it's doubly doubtful that you could do as good a job. One reason is that the best arrow shafts aren't lathe-turned but usually are planed to shape, then *ground* smooth. Conventional turning loosens the fibers, reduces the spine, and ordinarily produces warped arrows. (Most shaft-making machines, by the way, are designed by the manufacturers who use them, and the companies are reluctant to give away much information.)

In case you want to try making your own shafts (particularly those of off-parallel shape—barreled, for example), here's how old-timers still occasionally do it: Use straight-grained Douglas fir, Norway pine, birch or Port Orford cedar. Start with boards a half inch square and about three inches longer than your completed arrow length. Plane them down to a square board just a hair larger than the fattest diameter of your hoped-for-shaft.

With an extremely sharp plane—half-round molding plane, if you have one; a flat plane if not—begin smoothing the arrow, resting the end against a small block or holding it in a vise by the extra wood on the end. Arrange your work so the shaft rests full length on the workbench top.

Shave each corner to form an octagon, then smooth the shaft until a cylinder is produced, with whatever taper you want. A lathe capable of revolving at a very slow speed will help sand it down. Finish by sanding with the finest paper you can find, preferably checking diameter with a micrometer. In addition, weigh each shaft on a photo darkroom-type scale until you get a set matched as closely as practical. Acceptable tolerance is about 20 grains. Because the wood making up different parts of a board grows at varying rates, resulting in non-uniform densities, the shafts won't be exactly the same in both size and weight.

Unless you are a real workshop bug, however, better buy completed shafts. They're cheap, perfectly round, and matched for spine. Tell the dealer your arrow length and bow weight so he can select the right spine for you. Diameter varies with bow weight, as listed here:

Diameter	Bow Weight
9/32 in...................	To 30 lbs.
5/16 in...................	30 to 45 lbs.
11/32 in..................	45 to 70 lbs.
3/8 in...................	70 lbs. and up

How many shafts should you buy? Two dozen is a good number, if you're making your first try. From these you may salvage eight or ten good arrows. If you pick up the shafts at your local store, sight along each while spinning it between your fingers or rolling it along a glass counter top.

At home as you work with the shafts you'll find that some of them develop curves. Straighten the bent shafts as best you can by holding them over a stove until quite hot, then bending them in the opposite direction and holding them in this position until cool. You may find it practical to wedge the dowels under books or some other weight to hold them in this reverse-bent position.

Inevitably, a couple of shafts will remain obviously warped. Toss these on the scrap heap. Then take a few more of your most bent shafts and toss them out, too. You now have maybe eighteen with which to work.

First step in actual construction is the attachment of nocks —an easy job with today's ready-made, inexpensive plastic nocks. (Used to be that you had to cut slots into the arrow ends—providing excellent places for splits to start.)

Nocks are molded with tapered insides, so your dowel must taper to fit. For this use an 11° taper tool, a gadget that works like a pencil sharpener, but unlike nearly all pencil sharpeners (which should not be used), it makes an even taper. These tools cost about $2. Universal tool sets for tapering all shaft diameters cost somewhere between $5 and $10. Don't taper the dowel all the way to a point, but leave a small flat on the end; most nock holes stop just before coming to a point.

When all shafts are tapered, glue on the nocks with a cellulose-based plastic cement—model airplane glue, for example, or Borden's Casco Waterproof. Apply glue to the nock hole rather than to the shaft; not so much squishes out that way.

While the cement is still wet, the nock should be twisted around so that when the slot is vertical (as when the arrow is in the bow), the dowel's *flat grain* is on the top and bottom, *end grain* at sides. Arrows have more spine uniformity "edgewise," and because the major flexation of an arrow is around the bow, placing each arrow's edge grain against the bow leads to more all-round flight uniformity. Flat grain looks like feathery V's, something like deltas on a topographic map. To ease the twisting of the nock, pound a nail partially into your workbench top and slip the nock slot over it. Twist the arrows until the flat grain is up.

While the nocks are drying (20 minutes or so), mark and cut your arrows to your draw length. Measure from the base of the string notch, adding another inch and a half if the shafts are to be used for broadheads. Marking is easier if you line up the shafts, then with a rule as a guide, run a pencil along the whole batch.

The cut and nocked shafts are now smoothed with No. 0 garnet paper, followed by No. 00, then by very fine—the finest you can get—steel wool.

When smoothed, finish the shafts with varnish or good quality lacquer. The easiest way is dipping the whole shaft into the finish. A good container for this operation consists of a ½-inch (inside diameter) pipe, 30 inches long. Thread it on both ends and hold it up by a pipe flange screwed to a board of sufficient size that the pipe doesn't tip over. Before attaching the pipe to the board, ram a cork or tapered dowel into the bottom end so the paint doesn't run out. Before filling for the first time, pour a thimbleful of paint or varnish into the tube, then pour it out. Hardened, this will calk the bottom. With a pipe cap screwed on top, paint can be kept in the container.

Two coats, with a generous sanding and steel-wooling between, will cover an arrow sufficiently. Use clothespins to hang the arrows by their nocks to dry. A 2- by 4-inch board with holes drilled not quite through makes a good drying rack.

Now for fletching—the tough part. You can make it considerably easier on yourself by buying ready-cut feathers, available packaged by the dozen. Trueflight Mfg. Co. of Manitowish Waters, Wisconsin, for example, offers die-cut feathers running from fifty cents to $1.10 a dozen, depending on size and quality.

Ancient kings used peacock feathers, despite the fact that they weren't very good for arrows. Old British books on archery recommend gray goose feathers, but the reason is that nothing better was then available to the English. Today turkey feathers are used almost exclusively, tom feathers being preferred over hens because they are heavier and longer lasting.

Each bird donates to the sport of archery only the large pinion feathers from each wing tip. Cured by air-drying for about a month, the feathers are washed, dried, then split down the quill, for only the large half of each is usable. The quill base then is ground either flat or slightly concave to fit the shaft.

Every feather has an oil line, a padded section on the vane, more readily seen on the concave side. It runs from near the quill end, sweeps in a parabolic curve upwards and back on the vane, then dips sharply toward the rear. A feather with a fairly heavy oil line is preferred, for it indicates flexibility. Only the section below this line (between the line and the base) is used. Depending on the size, one hunting vane or two target vanes can be cut from each feather.

One point in feather selection is vital: tom or hen feathers and right- and left-hand feathers should not be mixed— neither on a single arrow, nor in a single set. In fact, it's a good idea to make a standing rule to use only right-hand (or left) toms; that way your fletching on one arrow set will be the same as that on another, and arrows may be interchanged. All feathers are labeled as to sex and side, so there is no problem.

If your plan includes ready-trimmed and dyed feathers, skip the following six paragraphs; they're applicable only to the man who wants to start from scratch.

First step is the dyeing of the so-called cock feathers, unless your batch has enough offbeat ones so that the cocks readily can be seen. Standard clothes dye can be used. Dyeing works best if the feathers are first soaked awhile in cold water, then swished around in a dishpan of dye, then back into the fresh water again to rinse off the excess coloring. If the hue is too light, swish around again. They can be dried in a home clothes dryer if the holes in the tumbler aren't so large the feathers can work themselves through.

Use your worst-looking full feather for the first try at trimming; you'll probably foul things up. First, snip off the useless small side of the feather and the fluffy top.

Next step: quill-slicing. You'll need an extremely sharp knife to do a good job—a safety razor blade, an X-Acto knife, or a fine jackknife honed to a sparkling edge. Resharpen the knife after each half-dozen feathers.

Lay the feather on a table, concave side up. Grasp your knife so the blade lies flat, parallel to the tabletop. Holding the quill firm on the surface, slice through it flatwise, cutting just low enough so that the groove inside the rib is exposed. Try to do it in one stroke, but if you can't, make little follow-up slices. When the quill is trimmed flat, the feather again is held to the table, but the knife blade comes in vertically. Slice close to the vane, tilting the knife ever so slightly so a little sliver of rib is left for the glue to stick to.

Some fletchers make their first cut with scissors, splitting the quill in half. Then they pare away the excess with a razor blade, starting at the point (heavy end) and working close enough to the feathery section so that no thick matter is left, yet not so close that the web is cut.

The feather is finished by placing it in some kind of vise— a clamp-type clip or commercial fletching jig—and working it smooth with very fine sandpaper.

Now that those who have bought ready-cut feathers are back with us, another painstaking process comes to the fore: positioning and gluing the feathers to the shaft. If they are slightly curled (most of them are), place the feathers between a couple of warm, damp cloths for a half hour. This takes out much of the curl, making lineup easier. Some fletchers claim they get even better results by dipping a towel in boiling water, wringing it out (wearing rubber gloves), folding the steaming towel over the feathers and weighting them with a board. Seems a bit rough, but some swear by it. Flattened this way, feathers can be dried before positioning; lets the glue grab hold. Also for better glue stickage, scrape the shaft paint a little where the feathers are to go.

The best thing for attaching feathers is a fletching jig. These cost anywhere from about $1 to $12 or so. You'll be happier with a better one. Jigs hold feathers at the correct angle (adjustable for straight or spiral installation), and usually have snap-in spots for 120-degree rotation of the shafts, assuring feather equidistance. (For the mass producer, batteries of 60 or more jigs are used by a single workman.)

Where are the feathers placed? This varies among archers, but the top of the feather usually falls about an inch below the bottom of the nock—give or take a quarter inch. As to whether or not feathers should be spiraled, that's an argument which hasn't been settled in the last thousand years. Spiraling—which imparts spin—does give stability in flight, does make the arrow fly straight. Of that, there's no doubt. But trouble comes, say those who prefer straight fletching, just after the arrow leaves the bow—before that spin starts. Spiraling throws it off kilter, say they. It's pretty well agreed, however, that broadheads do require a moderate spin— enough to make a revolution every ten feet or so to counteract planing.

Because feathers have a natural curve, and because they are highest at the back, they form a natural spiral anyway and subsequently spin the arrow in flight, albeit slowly. For the beginning arrowsmith—particularly if he is working on non-hunting missiles—straight fletching is easier.

With a mechanical fletcher, spiraled fletching is just as easy as straight: Simply clamp the arrow in the clip, spread a thin film of glue on the edge, and swing it over the arrow. Position it so that the upper tip of the cock feather is directly under the nock bump, 90 degrees from the string groove.

The man without a fletching gadget must use his eye. First he marks the shafts (by lining them up again so he can mark all in a single ruler-guided sweep), then wipes a little fletcher's cement on the feathers, lets it dry there to act as sizing.

Working without a jig necessitates pinning feathers in place, preferably with short, round-headed, sharp-pointed fletching pins. Regular dressmaking pins will do, however, as will black-headed milliner or map pins. Before positioning, each feather is pinned through each end, then most fletchers position the feathers (almost always three) as a team. Work on a board resting flat on the table—a board thick enough for the arrow to lie with its feathers sticking out over the edge. Place the arrow with the feather end away from you, and rest the pile end on your chest or stomach.

With the pins in the feathers—one at each end—catch the nock-end pin on the arrow, so positioned that the feather tip falls the correct distance from the nock. The cock feather, remember, falls directly under the nock bump, at right angles to the string groove. If you want spiral, the bottom (front) edge of the feather will be angled *away* from the concave side (inside) of the feather, about ⅛ inch around the shaft, the direction of rotation depending on whether you use right- or left-hand feathers.

Catch the pin nearest you in the wood, holding it at an angle pointing toward you, and as you push it in, pull it upright so as to straighten the feather and pull out the natural curve. The other two feathers are pinned on in the same manner. (Some nocks have corners on the bottom. If yours do, use these to line up your hen feathers.) Sight the feathers down from the nock to see that they form an equilateral triangle—easy to judge with a little practice. Also, see that each rises from the shaft at 90°, and that all are spiraled alike, if spiraled at all.

When the whole set is pinned, take the glue and run along each feather-shaft junction on each side, squeezing lightly and evenly. Make sure no glue accidentally wipes onto the vanes themselves. Let the arrows dry for a half hour or so, then put on a second coat. Pins can be removed in about an hour. Watch that feathers don't start to curl during drying time. If they do, push them straight.

Some archers have had magnificent results with contact cement. The big advantage is that you can work as fast as you like—no need to wait for the cement to harden. One user claims that he lost an arrow in the brush for two months, yet despite heavy rainfalls, no contact-cemented feathers were loose. This cement does, however, have a tendency to discolor the shaft.

Final feather operation is the shaping. Three methods are used: knife-and-template, die, and hot wire. Many shapes are in use, and for distinction you may even want to design your own.

Knife-and-template is the oldest method. The feather outline is cut from a piece of sheet metal, then with the arrow resting on the edge of a board, the feather is held down with the template and sheared off with a well-honed knife or razor blade. An adaptation is the double template, a pair of hinged metal plates which enclose the vane allowing only the waste edge to stick out.

Dies make the job easier. Occasionally they're available in archery shops, but most arrowsmiths who use them make their own. Use metal somewhat heavier than tin-can gauge —perhaps a strip tin-snipped from an oil drum. Hammer this into a cutting edge the desired shape of your feather—something like a cookie cutter. The edge must be sharp enough to cut with hand pressure, without the use of a mallet. Fashion a grooved block of wood to act as a presser-bar.

Best method of all—and something you should plan to purchase if you're serious about arrow making—is a hot-wire trimmer. Such a gadget may stink up your workroom from burning feathers, but the odor is a small price for ease of operation. Archery dealers sell these electrically operated jigs for as little as $2.50, as much as $25.

Basically, hot-wire trimmers consist of nicrome resistance wire—like a toaster wire—bent to the shape of the feather and heated red-hot by household current. Trimming with it is a snap: with the arrow nock resting in a rotary holder, the shaft is twisted so each feather contacts the nicrome and is burned off in the shape of the wire. (An occasional arrow builder complains that the heat burns out oil at the exposed edge, resulting in quick fraying; but the complaint is rare.) Be sure to keep the wire clean. One caution: shape the feather quickly, else it might burst into flame. Woe, woe.

After trimming, remove charred edges with fine sandpaper and taper the leading feather edges with a small, razory knife so they blend smoothly with the wood. A dab of cement applied at the leading edges will add strength to these vulnerable spots. Smooth it down when dried.

Putting heads on arrows is nearly as easy as securing the nocks. Arrowsmiths used to make their own heads, but mass production processes now grind out heads in such a profusion of styles at so low a price (from 50¢ a dozen for target points to $3 each for heavy-duty fish spears) that it just doesn't pay to fashion your own anymore.

Many points have cone-shaped insides, so a $5°$ pile taperer —similar to the pencil-sharpener-like nock-taper tool—is required for a good fit. Again, don't use a pencil sharpener or you'll invariably get a lopsided taper.

Parallel piles—so called because the inner and outer diameters are parallel except for the sharp, conical end—have walls $\frac{1}{32}$ of an inch thick. Therefore, if the pile-shoulder and arrow-shaft diameters are to be the same, the point end of the shaft must be reduced by $\frac{1}{16}$ of an inch. If a $\frac{5}{16}$-inch shaft is used, for example, its shoulder must be reduced to $\frac{1}{4}$ inch for use with a $\frac{5}{16}$-inch o.d. pile.

A "parallel pile" tennon tool simplifies the process. If none is available, try this method: With the arrow flat on your bench (feathers sticking over the edge) measure a distance from the end equal to the length of the pile's inside, then score it by rolling the shaft with the knife blade. Then using the knife and file, shave down the diameter. Take care not to cut too deeply at the shoulder; that will weaken the shaft.

Such difficulties can be bypassed by using the next larger size pile. (In the store, fit the shaft and pile together to make sure everything fits.) Main reason archers dislike using slip-on piles is that there is more likelihood that the head will come off in the target as the arrow is withdrawn. On the other hand, slip-over piles give added strength, particularly needed for field shooting.

Heads are fastened first by gluing, then by pricking one side with a hammer and nail, forming a hold-fast dent. (Two-bladed broadheads are placed so they are parallel with nocks' string grooves.) After gluing on non-hunting heads, some archers string their bows, fit the arrow and with a partial draw, let it fly against the floor. This drives home the point before the glue sets. It's important to make sure the arrow end fills the pile; if it doesn't, a strike on a rock in the field will slam it home, and perhaps split the shaft in the process. A good ploy here: Use a flexible ferrule cement—Casco's, for example. If the cement never sets really hard, it can better stand up under shock.

When heavier-than-usual casings are used they can be secured by wire brads. Drill a $\frac{1}{16}$-inch hole through each, dip a brad in glue, and tap it through so its head wedges in the pile hole. The pointed end is then cut off, and both sides filed smooth.

All that's left now is the crest. It makes the job look professional and identifies your arrows. The lazy man's way is to use commercial decals. A professional-looking home cresting job really requires use of a cresting lathe, a little too expensive for most archers' billfolds. For that reason, many homemade arrows are painted with an offbeat color of waterproof, quick-drying lacquer from the feathers down a few inches and let go at that. The handyman, however, can fashion a homemade cresting jig with a little imagination: a geared-down motor with a wedge-fit coupling to hold the arrow point, a short pin to hold the plastic nock steady, a rail on which to support the paintbrushes. Old phonograph turntable spindles revolve at just the right speed. A standard metal lathe, wood lathe or drill press can be used *if* it can be geared down far enough. One archer simply chucks arrow piles in a hand drill, squeezes the drill handle in a vise, and while he turns with one hand, paints with the other.

If you want to invest a little money—$20 or so—professional outfits can be had from mail-order houses or from local dealers on order.

When your arrows are dry, the big test comes—matching. You started with two dozen shafts, narrowed them down to 18, probably spoiled a few more, and have left, say, 15 beautifully designed missiles. For the test, number each arrow with a water-soluble ink or sharp grease pencil—something you can later remove.

Now, using your best form, shoot a few test rounds. Hopefully, the arrows will group in a fairly tight area. Some will be out of the picture, and some may have missed the target altogether—as expected.

As you withdraw each arrow, use the form on page ... to record where each arrow struck—3:00/5, 6:30/3, 12:00/7, etc.; the first number refers to the arrow's clock-face position, the second to the ring value. After you've shot around a dozen ends, you'll note on your chart that some arrows have a tendency to consistently hit in some areas, while others strike a different location each time. If any miss the target often, put them in a box by themselves. They're not much good except for rough practice. Those consistent only in their inconsistency also go into the practice box.

You should have eight or ten arrows left which group in a fairly tight area. These, then, are your masters, a matched set—six very fine missiles with two extras. You can be proud of them.

Renumber this matched set, using stick-on figures from your dealer or painting them on by hand. Cross out the no-good arrow columns on your chart, and substitute the new numbers in the appropriate columns. This gives you a permanent record (until feathers start to wear or shafts begin to warp) of flight characteristics of your entire set. A group that flies straight to the gold is ideal, of course, but few do. If the set bunches, say, at 10:00, you soon will automatically adjust for it, and your score will edge upward.

The making of arrows of aluminum and fiberglass follows pretty much the same pattern as the construction of wooden ones, except that a number of steps are skipped. Shaft selection and straightening, for example, pose no problem at all. Quality aluminum and fiberglass shafts are matched by the machines that turn them out. Nock and point cementing also presents no difficulty; most are of the slip-*in* type, are milled for perfect fit. For attaching feathers, however, a fletching jig is a necessity; no pins, of course, can be stuck into the shafting.

Some arrowsmiths feel that special cement is needed for glass and aluminum work; others do not. To be safe, you might as well use cement sold for the purpose—it costs about the same, anyway.

Homemade fiberglass or aluminum arrows still cost more than top quality store-bought wooden arrows, but by making your own non-wood missiles you can save a fair amount over commercially produced products. The standard price for a dozen finished aluminum arrows, for example, might average something more than $30, whereas if you put them together yourself you might save $10 or so. Typical list price of fiberglass target arrows is approximately $25 a dozen; you can probably fashion your own for about $16.

Large mail-order supply houses sell aluminum and fiberglass arrow-making sets. Best bet is to order at least your first batch as a set—you'll at least be sure everything is compatible.

Just one thing more on your homemade wooden arrows. Tests show that the very best ones become so by seasoning. If you want your set to be *really* fine, put them in storage for from seven to nine years. But I guess that's a bit much to ask.

ARROW NUMBER

1 2 3 4 5 6 7 8 9 10 11 12 13 14 15 16 17 18 19 20

R O U N D   N U M B E R

1
2
3
4
5
6
7
8
9
10

Chapter 20

IRRITATIONS, INJURIES, AND ACCIDENTS—HOW TO AVOID THEM

WHILE shooting on the shore of a northern Minnesota lake a few years ago, one of my arrows hit a rock. The point broke off, leaving a splintery, unrepairable shaft, so on impulse, I decided to try a flight shot out over the lake. Quickly I pulled back to full draw, let go—and the holler I loosed as the arrow bit into my hand shocked even the distant loons into silence.

I was no stranger to archery, yet I had pulled a classically stupid trick: overdraw. It hadn't occurred to me that the headless arrow was shortened, and that at full draw the splintered shaft would nestle my hand. Fortunately, after digging through that soft mound of flesh at the thumb/finger junction, the shaft glanced off the bone of my index finger. Had the arrow broken off a little shorter, it could have gone through my hand.

That arrow, retrieved from the beach (it was a very short flight) still sits in the corner of my den—a reminder that rules of safety are applicable not only to the raw novice.

Safety is a combination of common sense, knowledge of equipment, and experience, with a rule or two tossed in.

Though there are roughly a quarter million bowhunters in the woods each fall, archery accidents usually aren't so spectacular as those of firearms. In Wisconsin, for example, something like 15,000 bowhunters take to the field each year, yet there was not a single major reported mishap from 1934 to 1948, and no fatalities yet. Nevertheless, non-fatal "minor" accidents are quite common—even in Wisconsin. You don't hear of many of them simply because they reflect on the fatheadedness of the bowmen. And *they* don't like to talk.

In a single year, for example,

. . . A Michigan bowhunter, after bagging his deer, evened things up somewhat by sitting on a batch of three-bladed broadheads.

. . . A man in Florida, teaching his daughter how to draw in the front yard, surprised himself by sailing a slippery arrow through his newly installed picture window.

. . . A prospective deerslayer in New York dented his bow by closing the car door on it, decided to use it anyway, knocked himself cold when it broke.

. . . The gunstock of a hunter crouched in a thicket was split by a broadhead loosed by a bowman who thought he spied deer.

. . . While testing a new bow's draw weight, a Utah archer pinned his wife's foot to the living-room floor.

Equipment misuse and carelessness probably count for more archery troubles than any other aspect of the sport. The act of stringing, for example, can cause all sorts of nastiness if the bowman isn't on his toes. If the string is incorrectly nocked, it can slip off. If it slips during the draw the bow can break, whop the archer, and send the arrow Lord knows where. A neglected string that parts during the draw can cause the same thing. So can a string inadvertently wound up and shortened; for a too-high fistmele puts excessive pressure on both bow and string, either of which can snap. Cracks, splits, under-handle wrinkles, or separations of laminate materials are signs that the bow is straining, ready to let go. A sudden lowering of arrows on the target may also indicate bow senility. If any of these things happen to your bow, take it to an expert for repair before it breaks in two. If yours is an aluminum bow be especially watchful for fatigue cracks.

Such aggravations as sore fingers and forearm can be prevented by wearing fingertip and arm guards and holding the bow arm in a semi-relaxed position. If your fingertips hurt even with protectors, tincture of benzoin will help to toughen the skin. Incidentally, if the insides of your string fingers begin to blister, you may be squeezing your nock.

Overdrawing results from arrows either too long or too short—too long and the bow may break; too short, and the arrow tip can wedge in the belly of the bow, leading to inevitable breakage—of the arrow, the bow, or the hand. Stop others from drawing your bow. They wouldn't walk into your bathroom and try out your toothbrush.

One more quirk to keep in mind: The bow must be of the same approximate temperature as the air. Bows left lying in the hot summer sun, cooled enough to lower only the surface temperature, then shot, may shatter. Same thing with a bow brought in from an unheated garage in midwinter, then shot in the basement range. Let it warm up first. Fiberglass models are particularly vulnerable to temperature variations. A good habit to develop is to work slowly up to a full draw if the bow hasn't been shot recently: pull back a few inches, relax, pull back double the original amount, relax, etc.

For safety's sake, the cautious bowman will watch his arrows closely, too. On bows with no arrow rests, for example, a nasty finger puncture might result from a feather loose at the forward edge. The problem should be tackled from both directions: glue down all loose feathers, and install arrow rests on rest-less bows.

A few other things to keep in mind to protect yourself from injury:

1. When shagging arrows behind a field target, leave someone up front so followers know you're still around. When alone, lean your bow against the target. Conversely, when shooting on field courses, make sure no one has lingered behind the target. A holler of "Timber!" may seem foolish, but it could save a puncture. Keep mindful that the range of a modern bow is about that of a shotgun—200 yards or more.

2. It's a temptation, but never shoot an arrow straight up. You'll suddenly find that it has disappeared, and there's no place to hide.

3. Always follow the pathways on a field course. Shortcuts may cut short your archery days.

4. Seems an obvious thing to be aware of, but because the accident is so common, we'll list it: Watch yourself in your shop when working on broadheads; many is the bowhunter who missed the season because his hand was too heavily bandaged to hold a bow. Use a vise to hold broadheads at home, and carry a small, clamp-on model with you to camp. File by stroking from base to point so that you don't get it in the hand. Speaking of hand-slicing broadheads, bowhunters seem to have a propensity for cutting themselves while using knives to dig heads out of trees.

5. Ricocheting arrows can do odd things. Make it a personal rule never to stand close to a target, and never to shoot until everyone is behind you.

6. Indoor ranges should have no doors through which people can walk into the arrow paths. Install locks.

7. In tournaments, if contenders are to shoot concurrently at varying distances, stagger the targets, not the people. In other words, two targets could be placed at 50 yards, two at 60, two at 100, etc., measured from a common shooting line. The National Safety Council recommends six yards as the

minimum width range, while at least three yards should be allowed between targets.

8. Don't allow an amateur to string your bow unless you guide his every move.

Some 90 percent of all bowhunting accidents are self-inflicted and it has been found that the largest percentage of these result from stalking with a cocked arrow. Safety rules usually proclaim that the archer should never travel with an arrow in his bow, but few bowhunters concur. To be vigilant, a bowman on the hunt usually keeps an arrow on the ready, the bow tensed. We shouldn't, but we do.

What can happen? What *does* happen? Typical accident occurs when two hunters are stalking together, both arrows set. The first one hears a noise, stops, and the second rams him in the butt with his drawn arrow. Moral: Always be the last guy in line.

To those uninitiated in the vicissitudes of archery, the report that a bowhunter jabbed himself by falling on his own arrow is hilarious. Not to the man who has hunted with a bow; he remembers his own close calls. The hunter isn't paying particular attention to where he is stepping; he's looking for game, hardly to be found underfoot. Consequently, he might miss rocks, vines, or slippery places—and fall. Instinctively he throws out his arms and all too often the bow smacks a limb, turning the arrow toward the hunter.

Chances of injury are reduced if you carry your arrow in a bow quiver or parallel with and flat against the bow, held in place by the hand on the handle. But if you won't operate that way, at least be cautious. If every once in a while you stop to consider the worst possible thing that could happen, its ramifications might help you to play it safer.

Speaking of quivers, these cause a lot of trouble in the field. Razor-sharp broadheads easily can work themselves through shabbily made quivers bouncing along on your back. If the points stick out only a quarter-inch, a painful cut can result. A good idea is to fashion a cup of sheet metal for the quiver bottom; then, to protect the points, pad it with a layer or two of sponge rubber from an old kneeling pad.

If you're thinking of buying a bow quiver, check first to see that it doesn't allow the broadheads to be exposed, that they're protected with material so strong that you could fall on it without injury. Particularly dangerous are plastic quivers which leave the heads exposed. These may be subject to warping from contrasting temperatures, and the razory blades set only a few inches from the archer's face can cause serious injury if they jump out during a shot.

Cardinal rule in hunting safety is to make sure of your quarry before you bag it. Yet almost any experienced bowman can cite a number of close calls in which he almost got hit (never when he almost hit someone else). To be safe, don't shoot up a hill where a miss might mean a flight shot. If you are sitting in a blind and another hunter waltzes by, let him know you're there, even if it means scared game. Keep in mind too the increased hazard from ricocheting arrows in deep-wood hunting. Something else to contemplate: Crouched over and sneaking behind a row of foliage with your shoulder-quivered arrows silhouetted against the sky, you may very well look like an antlered buck to the rifleman on the next hill. So at least wear brightly colored clothing. And by the way, take it easy when you drag out your deer; you're not so young as you used to be.

Three other situations where you should be careful:

. . . When shooting up into a tree, take care you're not struck by your own arrow falling back. This situation resulted in a cut throat a few years ago.

. . . When stepping over logs, be particularly watchful that you don't jab yourself in the knee with your broadheads. This accident is quite common.

. . . If your broadhead gets entangled in the dense underbrush, don't, in irriation, jerk it out. We nearly lost one of our most famous bowhunters this way a few seasons ago.

The broadhead suddenly let go and zipped right through his hunting pants and into the back of the thigh.

Dozens of pages could be written about first-aid treatments. Past experience shows that few would read them, and fewer still would remember the rules. However, if every bowhunter who reads this remembers just one point, I guarantee saved lives over the years. The point is simply this: Use your finger to stop profuse bleeding. If you ram your broadhead into your thigh, forget about tourniquets; while someone runs for help, stick your finger onto the wound. If there are three in your party, one should go for a doctor while the second stays, with his finger, two fingers, or whole palm on the wound. Let the doctor worry about infections later. The immediate job: stop the bleeding.

Mishaps are nearly always the result of carelessness, thoughtlessness, or ignorance. The bow and arrow was the most effective warfare weapon for centuries. Scores of thousands of men have been killed by flying arrows, and modern bows are far more murderous.

Appendix

ARCHERY EQUIPMENT SUPPLIERS

The following list is for the convenience of the reader. The only reason these names appear and not others is simply that the author has some familiarity with the organizations. Most companies carry more than one type of product (almost no one handles bows only, for example), but where, in the author's opinion, an organization is known especially for a single type of product, that item is specified. Most companies offer catalogs.

Cedar arrow shafts
Acme Wood Products Co.
Myrtle Point, Oregon

Supply house
Anderson Archery Sales Co.
Grand Ledge, Michigan

Accessories
Bayou Manufacturing Co.
Box 5124
San Antonio 1, Texas

Bows
Bear Archery Co.
R.R. 1
Grayling, Michigan

Bows
Ben Pearson, Inc.
Pine Bluff, Arkansas

Bows
Birnie Bows
12429 No. Central Expressway
Dallas 31, Texas

Bows
Browning Arms Co.
Ogden, Utah

Bows
Colt's Patent Fire Arms Mfg.
    Co., Inc.
Hartford 15, Conn.

Aluminum arrow shafting
Jas. D. Easton, Inc.
15137 Califa Street
Van Nuys, California

Supply house
Herter's, Inc.
Waseca, Minnesota

Bows
Howatt Archery Mfg., Inc.
Route 8
Yakima, Washington

Bows
Hoyt Archery Company
11510 Natural Bridge
Bridgeton, Mo.

Supply house
Kinsey's Arrow Shop
Chocolate Avenue
Florin, Pa.

Supply house
Kittredge Bow Hut
1421 Mission
So. Pasadena, Calif.

Telescopic bowsights
Norland Associates, Inc.
Ft. Atkinson, Wisc.

Glass bows
Paul Bunyan Company
1030 Marshall St., N.E.
Minneapolis 13, Minn.

Supply house
The Robin Hood Archery Co.
215 Glenridge Avenue
Montclair, N. J.

Accessories
Rome Sporting Goods
104 John Street
Rome, N. Y.

Targets
Saunders Archery Target Co.
Box 102
Columbus, Nebraska

Bows
Shakespeare Company
R.F.D. No. 5 — Box 13
Kalamazoo, Michigan

Telescopic bowsights
SKA Scope Mount, Inc.
3721 Market Street
Spokane 27, Washington

Bows
L. E. Stemmler Co.
Manorville, Long Island, N. Y.

Bows
Tarbell Custom Bows
P. O. Box 429
Ontario, Calif.

Feathers
True Flight Mfg. Co., Inc.
Manitowish Waters, Wisc.

Supply house
L. C. Whiffen Co., Inc.
209 W. Wells St.
Milwaukee 3, Wisc.

Automatic indoors targets
West Coast Engineering
818 South Dakota St.
Seattle 8, Washington

Bows
Wing Archery Company
7106 Mapleridge
Houston 36, Texas

Bows
York Archery (Woodcraft
    Equip. Co.)
1450 West Lexington
Independence, Mo.

Arrowheads
Zwickey Archery Co.
2571 E. 12th Avenue
North St. Paul 9, Minn.

ASSOCIATIONS

National

American Bowhunters Association, Inc. (ABA)
Sportsman's Haven
Route 1
Alpena, Michigan

American Crossbow Association
Huntsville, Arkansas

Archery Institute
23 East Jackson Boulevard
Chicago 4, Illinois

Archery Manufacturers and Dealers Association (AMADA)
23 East Jackson Boulevard
Chicago 4, Illinois

National Archery Association (NAA)
23 East Jackson Boulevard
Chicago 4, Illinois

National Collegiate Archery Coaches Association
Louisiana Polytechnic Institute
Ruston, Louisiana

National Company of Crossbowmen
c/o Col. Francis E. Pierce
1024 Glorietta Blvd.
Coronado, Calif.

National Crossbowmen
c/o Fred Isles
10 Arlington Road
Cranford, N. J.

National Field Archery Association (NFAA)
Route 2, Box 514
Redlands, California

Professional Archers Association (PAA)
c/o Karl E. Palmatier
Route 1, Box 32
Hickory Corners, Michigan

International

le Fédération Internationale de Tir A l'Arc (FITA)
Federation of International Target Archers
c/o Mrs. Inger Frith
Fairfield, Copthorne Road
Croxley Green, Herts, England

British

Grand National Archery Society
c/o P. H. Bragg
Deaks Lane, Cuckfield
Sussex, England

British Field Archery Association
c/o P. Sonnicksen
37b Burnt Ash Road, Lee Green
London, SE 12, England

MAGAZINES

Many regional archery magazines and newspapers are born periodically, then wither away. National magazines, however, seem to stay comparatively healthy. Here are the four most vigorous, available by subscription or through organization memberships:

ARCHERY. Published monthly. Official publication of the National Field Archery Assn. Subscription: $2.50 per year in the U.S.; Canada, $2.75; all others, $3. Combination membership in NFAA and magazine: $5.00. Mail to Box H, Palm Springs, Calif.

ARCHERY WORLD (formerly *Bowhunting Magazine*). Published monthly. The official publication of the National Archery Association. Combined membership in NAA and subscription to magazine is $5 a year for an individual or a husband/wife couple. Those under 18 who join independent of family: $3. Send either to NAA, 23 East Jackson Blvd., Chicago 4, Illinois, or to *Archery World*, Riderwood, Md.

Bow & ARROW, the newest of the lot. (It began in 1963.) Round-up of both field and target archery, but leans toward field. Published bi-monthly for $3 a year. Address: 2935 Palau Place, Costa Mesa, Calif.

TAM—THE ARCHERS' MAGAZINE. Monthly. Leaning toward the professional archer, but not officially so. Subscription: $3 per year in the U.S., $3.50 elsewhere. Address: 33 E. Fourth Street, Boyertown, Pa.

In England, it's *The British Archer*, a bi-monthly magazine angled toward the target archer but also acknowledging the new (in England) sport of field archery. Cost is $3 a year, and address is 18 Lodge Avenue, Cosham, Portsmouth, England.

STATE GAME COMMISSIONS

Laws pertaining to hunting with bow and arrows vary considerably between states and from year to year. Archers planning to hunt should contact the appropriate authority listed below.

Alabama: Director, Division of Game, Fish and Seafoods, Department of Conservation, Montgomery 4.

Alaska: Commissioner, Department of Fish and Game, 229 Alaska Office Building, Juneau.

Arizona: Director, Game and Fish Department, Arizona State Building, Phoenix.

Arkansas: Director, Game and Fish Commission, Little Rock.

California: Director, Department of Fish and Game, 722 Capitol Ave., Sacramento 14.

Colorado: Director, Game and Fish Commission, 1530 Sherman Street, Denver 5.

Connecticut: Director, Board of Fisheries and Game, State Office Building, Hartford 14.

Delaware: Director, Board of Game and Fish Commissioners, Dover.

District of Columbia: Superintendent, Metropolitan Police, Washington.

Florida: Director, Game and Fresh Water Fish Commission, Tallahassee.

Georgia: Director, Game and Fish Commission, 401 State Capitol, Atlanta 3.

Hawaii: Fish and Game Division, Commissioner of Agriculture and Forestry, Honolulu.

Idaho: Director, Department of Fish and Game, Boise.

Illinois: Director, Department of Conservation, Springfield.

Indiana: Director, Division of Fish and Game, Department of Conservation, 311 West Washington Street, Indianapolis 9.

Iowa: Director, State Conservation Commission, East Seventh and Court Streets, Des Moines 9.

Kansas: Director, Forestry, Fish and Game Commission, Pratt.

Kentucky: Commissioner, Department of Fish and Wildlife Resources, Frankfort.

Louisiana: Secretary-Director, State Wildlife and Fisheries Commission, 126 Civil Courts Building, New Orleans 16.

Maine: Commissioner, Department of Inland Fisheries and Game, State House, Augusta.

Maryland: Director, Department of Game and Inland Fish, State Office Bldg., Annapolis.

Massachusetts: Director, Division of Fisheries and Game, 73 Tremont St., Boston 8.

Michigan: Director, Department of Conservation, Lansing 26.

Minnesota: Commissioner, Department of Conservation, State Office Building, St. Paul 1.

Mississippi: Director, Game and Fish Commission, P. O. Box 451, Jackson.

Missouri: Director, Conservation Commission, Farm Bureau Building, Jefferson City.

Montana: State Fish and Game Warden, Department of Fish and Game, Helena.

Nebraska: Director, Game Forestation and Parks Commission, Lincoln 29.

Nevada: Director, Fish and Game Commission, 51 Grove St., Reno.

New Hampshire: Director, Fish and Game Department, State House Annex, Concord.

New Jersey: Director, Department of Conservation and Economic Development, Division of Fish and Game, 230 W. State St., Trenton 7.

New Mexico: Director, Department of Game and Fish, Santa Fe.

New York: Commissioner, Conservation Department, Albany 7.

North Carolina: Executive Director, Wildlife Resources Commission, Raleigh.

North Dakota: Commissioner, Game and Fish Department, Capitol Building, Bismarck.

Ohio: Chief, Division of Wild Life, Department of Natural Resources, 1500 Dublin Road, Columbus 12.

Oklahoma: Director, Department of Wildlife Conservation, State Capitol Building, Room 118, Oklahoma City 5.

Oregon: State Game Director, State Game Commission, P. O. Box 4136, Portland 8.

Pennsylvania: Executive Director, Pennsylvania Game Commission, Harrisburg.

Rhode Island: Chief, Division of Fish and Game, Department of Agriculture and Conservation, State House, Providence 2.

South Carolina: Director, Wildlife Resources Department, Box 360, Columbia.

South Dakota: Director, Department of Game, Fish and Parks, Pierre.

Tennessee: Director, Tennessee Game and Fish Commission, Cordell Hull Bldg., Nashville 3.

Texas: Executive Secretary, Game and Fish Commission, Austin.

Utah: Director, Fish and Game Commission, 1596 West North Temple, Salt Lake City 16.

Vermont: Director, Fish and Game Commission, Montpelier.

Virginia: Executive Director, Commission of Game and Inland Fisheries, P. O. Box 1642, Richmond 13.

Washington: Director, Department of Game, 600 N. Capitol Way, Olympia.

West Virginia: Director, Conservation Commission of West Virginia, Charleston.

Wisconsin: Director, Conservation Department, State Office Building, Madison 1.

Wyoming: State Game and Fish Commissioner, Wyoming Game and Fish Commission, Cheyenne.

Canada: Chief, Canadian Wildlife Service, Ottawa.

Alberta: Fish and Game Commissioner, Department of Lands and Forests, Edmonton.

British Columbia: Game Commissioner, Office of Game Commission, 567 Burrard Street, Vancouver.

Manitoba: Director of Game and Fisheries Branch, Department of Mines and Natural Resources, Winnipeg.

New Brunswick: Chief, Fish and Wildlife Branch, Department of Lands and Mines, Fredericton.

Newfoundland: Director, Wildlife Division, Department of Mines and Resources, P. O. Box 127, St. Johns.

Northwest Territories: Deputy Commissioner of N. W. T., Vimy Bldg., Ottawa.

Nova Scotia: Department of Lands and Forests, 513 Prince St., Truro.

Ontario: Chief, Fish and Wildlife Division, Department of Lands and Forests, Toronto 2.

Prince Edward Island: Deputy Minister of Industry and Natural Resources, Charlottetown.

Province of Quebec: General Superintendent, Department of Game and Fish, Quebec.

Saskatchewan: Game Commissioner, Department of Natural Resources, Saskatchewan Resources Building, Regina.

Yukon Territory: Commissioner, Yukon Territory, White Horse, Y. T.

Mexico: Secretaria de Agricultura y Ganaderia, Direccion General Forestal y de Caza, México, D. F.

Puerto Rico: Department of Agriculture and Commerce, Division of Fisheries and Wildlife, San Juan.

MODEL CONSTITUTION

For Field Archery Clubs

Courtesy, NATIONAL FIELD ARCHERY ASSOCIATION

CONSTITUTION OF

_____

(NAME OF CLUB)

ARTICLE I

The name of this organization shall be _____

_____.

ARTICLE II

Purpose

1. The purpose of this organization shall be:

To foster, expand, and perpetuate the practice of field archery, and the spirit of good fellowship among all archers; to encourage the use of the bow in hunting of all legal game, birds, and animals, and cooperate with the National Field Archery Association in securing better hunting privileges and conditions for bow hunters; to cooperate with all conservation organizations in the conservation of game; to maintain a field course and conduct field tournaments and games in accordance with the rules of the National Field Archery Association.

ARTICLE III

Membership

1. Active membership shall be granted to anyone who has attained his sixteenth birthday, upon application and payment of regular fees and dues and upon approval of the Secretary as to good moral character and sportsmanship.

2. Junior membership shall be granted to anyone under sixteen years of age upon payment of such fees and dues as may be fixed by the Board of Directors.

3. The Board of Directors may suspend or expel any member for conduct detrimental to the interests of the organization.

ARTICLE IV

Board of Directors

1. The Board of Directors shall consist of a President, Vice-President, and Secretary and Treasurer (office combined), and two regular members.

2. The Board of Directors shall control and manage the activities, policies, and property of the organization.

3. At any meeting of the Board three members of the Board shall constitute a quorum.

4. All vacancies of the Board on any office shall be filled by appointment by the Board of Directors.

5. The Board of Directors shall meet at least once a month at a time and place fixed by the Board.

ARTICLE V

Officers and Their Duties

1. The officers of this organization shall consist of a President, Vice-President, and a Secretary and Treasurer (office combined).

2. The President shall preside at all meetings, appoint all committees and shall in general perform the duties incident to his office.

3. The Vice-President shall perform the duties of the President if he is unable to act.

4. The Secretary shall keep all records of the organization, serve all notices of meetings, conduct all correspondence, and present a written report at the annual meeting, and in general perform all duties incident to his office.

5. The Treasurer shall receive all moneys of the organization. He shall keep accurate records of the receipts and disbursements and make an annual written report at the annual meeting, and in general have the powers to perform the duties incident to his office.

ARTICLE VI

Election and Terms of Office

1. The annual meeting of this organization shall be held on . . . . . .
. . . . (preferably at the end of the year's activities or sufficient time before beginning of year's activities so following year's activities can be well planned.)

2. At the annual meeting the membership shall elect the President, Vice-President, and the Secretary-Treasurer (office combined).

3. At the first annual meeting the membership shall elect two directors, the one receiving the highest number of votes shall serve for two years, the one receiving the second highest number of votes for a period of one year. Thereafter, the directors shall be elected for a term of two years.

ARTICLE VII

Fees and Dues

1. The membership fee for active members shall be $———————— per year for single persons, $———————— per year for a family membership. The junior membership fee shall be fixed by the Board of Directors.

2. Target fees and tournament fees shall be fixed by the Board of Directors.

ARTICLE VIII

Fiscal Year

1. The fiscal year of the organization shall begin ——————————
——————————, 19———, (day following annual meeting).

ARTICLE IX
Committees

1. The President shall appoint committees of three or more persons as follows: Constitution, Grounds, Membership, Tournament, Publicity, Conservation, Ladies, and special committees as may be necessary.

ARTICLE X
Tournaments

1. An annual tournament to determine the field archery championship of the organization and other tournaments shall be held as determined by the Board of Directors.

2. All championship tournaments shall be in accordance with the rules of the National Field Archery Association.

ARTICLE XI
Amendments

1. This Constitution may be amended by a two-thirds vote of the membership at any annual meeting or special meeting called for that purpose.

BY-LAWS

If the club desires more detailed or special provisions for carrying out or amplifying the various articles of the Constitution, or matters not provided for in the Constitution, they can be more specifically provided for in the By-Laws. Each club will have its own problems, and can adopt or add to its own By-Laws provisions from time to time as needed.

GLOSSARY

Anchor	The spot on the face or neck where the string hand rests at time of release.
Arm	See *limb*.
Armguard	Piece of leather wrapped around the forearm to protect from string slap.
Arrow plate	Vertical section of the bow against which the arrow rests before release.

Arrow rest	Shelf or projection upon which the arrow rests and slides when released.
Back	Side of the bow facing the target.
Backed bow	Bow which has a layer of material (plastic, for example) glued to the back for reinforcement.
Bare bow	No sights or other aiming devices.
Barreled arrow	Arrow thickest at the center and tapering toward each end.
Belly	Side of the bow facing the archer.
Bowyer	A bow maker.
Bow weight	The force in pounds needed to pull the bow to full draw.
Brace	To string a bow; also, see *armguard*.
Bobtailed arrow	Arrow thicker at the pile than at the nock.
Bodkin	Long, three-bladed broadhead.
Bolt	Crossbow arrow.
Broadhead	Triangular-shaped, sharp and flat hunting head.
Butt	Backstop for target face or matt—straw bale, for example.
Cast	The speed or distance a bow can shoot.
Chested arrow	Arrow thickest near the nock, tapering both toward the nock and pile. (Also *breasted*).
Clout target	Standard four-foot target enlarged 12 times and laid flat on the ground, shot at a distance of 180 yards.
Cock feather	Usually of a different color; always at right angles to string.
Creep	The edging forward of the arrow during aiming.
Composite bow	Bow made of more than one kind of material, e.g., maple and fiberglass.
Crest	Painted rings of varying colors and sizes near the feathers of an arrow for identification.
Dart	See *bolt*.
Double Round	Any round shot twice in succession and the scores added.
Draw	Hauling back on the bowstring.
Drawing weight	See *bow weight*.
Drift	The sideways movement of an arrow due to cross-wind.
End	In American target competition, 6 arrows shot at a target.
Eye	Loop on the end of a bowstring.

Face	Target front.
Facing	Material glued to the bow's belly for strength.
Finger stall	Leather finger tips to protect the draw fingers.
Fistmele	Distance from the belly of a bow to the string.
Fletch	To put feathers on an arrow.
Fletcher	An arrowsmith.
Fletching	The feathers or vanes on an arrow.
Flight arrow	An arrow made for distance shooting.
Flirt	A flicking or jerking of the arrow, particularly just after it leaves the bow.
Follow the string	Said of a bow which has taken a permanent set in the draw direction.
Foot bow	Flight bow set against the feet and drawn with both hands.
Footed arrow	Arrow with a piece of hardwood set into the pile end for strength.
Flu-flu (floo-floo)	Used for bird shooting; fletching is so large that drag causes short flight.
Free style	Anything goes.
Gold	Bull's-eye.
Grip	Bow handle.
Hen feathers	On a three-feathered arrow, the two that are colored alike.
Hold	The pause at full draw.
In	In field archery, second unit (loop) shot in a round: the *in* unit.
Kick	Jar felt when a poor bow is loosed.
Kisser	Knot or small button in string against which the lips are pressed to fix draw and arrow elevation.
Lay the body in the bow	Old English, meaning that the whole upper body, not just the arm muscles, should be used in the draw.
Let down	Loss of bow weight.
Limb	Sections of bow above or below handle.
Longbow	Straight bow of more than five feet, specifically bows of old as used in medieval England.
Loose	Releasing the drawn string.
Matt	Target boss, ordinarily the straw or grass coil onto which the target is placed.
Nock	Notch or groove into which the bowstring fits, either on the arrow or the limb tips; the placing of the string into the arrow slot.

Nocking point	Spot on the string where the arrow nock fits, often designated by extra serving.
Out	In field archery, first unit to be shot in a round.
Overbowed	Bow too difficult to draw for one's strength.
Overstrung	Too high fistmele caused by short string.
Petticoat	White, scoreless edge of a target.
Pile (pyle)	Arrowhead without a sharp, hunting edge.
Pin hole (pimple)	Aiming spot in center of target.
Pluck	To jerk with the hand at loose.
Point	Pile.
Point-blank	Distance from target at which the point-of-aim and gold coincide.
Point-of-aim	Object upon which an archer sights in order to achieve correct elevation.
Range finder	Aid to finding target distance or for determining point-of-aim.
Recurved bow	Bow with its tips formed with a reverse bend.
Reflex bow	Bow with limbs curving away from the archer when unstrung and held in shooting position.
Release	Loose.
Riser	Extra strip or block of wood glued to the belly side of a bow's handle for reinforcement or depth.
Round	Certain number of arrows shot at given distances; e.g., American Round is 30 arrows (in ends of 6) shot at 60, 50, and 40 yards, 90 in all: In field shooting a two-unit or 28-target course.
Rover	One who practices roving or the old method of field archery: shooting progressively at casual targets, e.g., stumps.
Self	Made of a single kind of material—an arrow with no footing or a bow of only one species of wood, without fiberglass.
Serving	Extra thread wrapped around the bowstring for longer wear.
Shaftment	Part of the arrow shaft to which feathers are attached.
Spine	In arrows, combination of firmness, stiffness and elasticity; the ability to return to original shape after bending around the bow when released.
Stake	Designates shooting position in field archery.
Tab	One- or two-holed leather patch with string slot to protect the drawing fingers.

Tackle	Archery equipment.
Tiller	Verb meaning to find the curvature of a bow at all bends and to correct unequal bending.
Toxophilite	Archery enthusiast (from Greek *toxon*, bow and *philos*, loving).
Underbowed	One with a too-weak bow for his strength.
Unit	Half of a full field course, a fourteen-target loop.
Vane	Fletching, usually said of plastic.
Walk-up	Progressive shooting stakes and a single target.
Wand	A board two inches wide, six feet long, stuck in the ground, used as a target.
Weight	See *bow weight*.

BIBLIOGRAPHY

Of the hundreds of books published on archery since *Toxophilus*, these are the ones I've found most valuable:

Ascham, Roger, *Toxophilus*, 1868 (original 1545), London: A. Murray & Son.

Burke, Edmund, *Field and Target Archery*, 1961, New York: Arco Publishing Company, Inc.

Burke, Edmund, *The History of Archery*, 1957, New York: William Morrow and Company.

Elmer, Robert P., *Archery*, 1926, Philadelphia: The Penn Publishing Company.

Elmer, Robert P., *Target Archery*, 1946, New York: Alfred A. Knopf.

Forbes, Thomas, *New Guide to Better Archery*, 1962, New York: Collier Books.

Herter, George L. and Hofmeister, Russell, *Professional and Amateur Archery*, 1963, Waseca, Minnesota: Herter's, Inc.

Hill, Howard, *Archery Adventures* (originally *Hunting the Hard Way*), 1955, Los Angeles: Trend, Incorporated.

Hodgkin, Adrian E., *The Archer's Craft*, 1951, London: Faber & Faber; New York: A. S. Barnes and Company.

Hougham, Paul, *The Encyclopedia of Archery*, 1958, New York: A. S. Barnes & Company.

National Field Archery Association, *Official Handbook, Field Archery*, 1963, Redlands, Calif.: NFAA.

Perry, Walter, *Bucks and Bows*, 1953, Harrisburg: The Telegraph Press.

Pope, Saxton T., *Bows and Arrows* (originally *A Study of Bows and Arrows*), 1962 (original 1923), Berkeley: University of California Press.

Stalker, Tracy L., *How to Make Modern Archery Tackle*, 1954, Flint, Michigan (4221 Springfield St.): Privately printed by Tracy Stalker.

Stemmler, Louis E., *Essentials of Archery*, 1956, Manorville, L. I., N. Y.: L. E. Stemmler Co.

Thompson, Maurice, *The Witchery of Archery*, 1928 (original 1878), Pinehurst, N. C.: The Archers Co.

Also recommended are the various catalogs published by the larger archery equipment supply houses, e.g., Robin Hood of Montclair, N. J.; Kinsey's of Florin, Pa.; and Kittredge Bow Hut of Pasadena, Calif. *Ishi in Two Worlds*, by Theodora Kroeber (1961, Berkeley and Los Angeles: University of California Press) is also interesting for discussions of primitive bows and arrows.

Index

251